Hosea Model for Marriage

A Biblical Model for Marriage Relationships

By

Glenn J. Miller

RAGGED EDGE PRESS

This Ragged Edge Press publication
was printed by
Beidel Printing House, Inc.
63 West Burd Street
Shippensburg, PA 17257-0152 USA

In respect for the scholarship contained herein, the acid-free paper used in this book meets the guidelines for permanence and durability of the Committee on Production Guidelines for Book Longevity of the Council on Library Resources.

For a complete list of available publications
please write
Ragged Edge Press
Division of White Mane Publishing Company, Inc.
P.O. Box 152
Shippensburg, PA 17257-0152 USA

Library of Congress Cataloging-in-Publication Data

Miller, Glenn I., 1942–
    Hosea model for marriage : a biblical model for marriage
relationships / by Glenn I. Miller.
        p.   cm.
    ISBN 1-57249-121-3 (alk. paper)
    1. Bible. O.T. Hosea--Criticism, interpretation, etc.
    2. Marriage--Religious aspects--Christianity.   3. Marriage--Biblical
teaching.   I. Title.
    BS1565.6.M3M55   1998
    248.4--dc21   98-4015
                                                                      CIP

This book is dedicated to my wife, Betty—
my helpmate, life partner, truest critic, and
closest friend

CONTENTS

The parallels implied in the relationship of marriage and their effect upon other kinds of relationships are explored. The communication process in relation to marriage and other relationships is also discussed. How the Hosea model points to the parallel that exists between marriage and other relationships.

A focus on finding relationship models that work and are worthy of emulation. Creating the right atmosphere, establishing specific priorities, and maintaining certain habits are looked at in terms of making marriage relationships healthier and stronger.

PREFACE

Marriage and family counseling have consistently been a major focus in my professional training and work. Having spent twenty years as a navy chaplain, I found myself ministering to persons directly and indirectly affected by personal relationships. I served with three different sea services (the navy, the marine corps, and the coast guard). In the process, I discovered that the human problems and concerns encountered by military personnel and families, regardless of branch of service, were very much the same. Among these problems and concerns, personal relationship issues, particularly interpersonal relationship issues, were paramount.

As a Christian, I believe the truth of God's word provides guidance, help, and real answers to the dilemmas and problems people face. I also believe the models of marriage found in both Jewish and Christian Scriptures describing God's relationship to his people and Christ's relationship to the Church are far from accidental. Both scripture and human experience present marriage as the most intimate and personal of human relationships. The relationship of marriage is a vehicle which can serve to enhance our relationship with God; it also can serve to enhance our human relationships. This is the primary point behind this book.

Although this work contains examples from military life, it is not specifically written for a military audience. Although this book concerns the relationship of marriage, it is not exclusively written for people who are married. And though it is true this work is based on a biblical model and is written from a Christian perspective, it provides information, insights, and tools concerning relationship formation and building which are applicable and suitable for general audiences.

Much of the material for this book was presented in abstract format in a scheduled presentation at the American Association of Christian Counselors Regional Conference, held in the Washington D.C. Metro Area, on 8–9 March 1996. Many of the questions, remarks, and comments I received, both during and following the presentation, indicated a very favorable response. Only one individual verbalized disagreement with my interpretation of Hosea. His comments became the focus of a rally of defense by many others on the appropriateness and relevancy of the material I presented.

The health and condition of today's marriage relationships are of increasing concern for many people. Material providing effective guidelines and useful tools applicable to such relationships have become actively sought after. For those open to God's guidance and direction on the matter, scripturally based insight are particularly helpful and important. On a personal level, when I have shared with colleagues and clients the fact I am writing this kind of book, I have encountered enthusiastic feedback and response. For these reasons I know a readership exists for the kind of manuscript I have written.

Hosea Model for Marriage: A Biblical Model for Marriage Relationships may be similar to other evangelical books on marriage in regards to the importance of marriage commitment, acknowledging God's presence and grace in persons' lives, and providing tools to help measure and evaluate the wellness and wholeness of marriage relationships. It is unlike other books on marriage in its reliance on and presentation of one particular biblical model found within the book of Hosea. Of the numerous examples used to illustrate the four truths concerning relationships found within this model, many come from my own ministry with military families.

Although military deployments, separations, and frequent moves place special stress and strain on military families, the marriage problems and issues encountered are not very different from those faced by civilian families. The tools presented in this book to help strengthen and enhance the relationship of marriage are useful and appropriate for any person seriously considering marriage or who is already married. Such tools have been field tested many times in workshops, in seminars, and in counseling sessions on premarriage and marriage that I have conducted for couples and individuals in various churches, chapels, bases, and classrooms in the United States and overseas.

INTRODUCTION

This is not another "how to" book. There are certainly enough of those already in print. I offer no special ingredient, magic formula, or distinctive elixir that guarantees to provide a successful relationship and a lasting marriage. However, this book *does* point to a biblical model for marriage. It is a model that provides the reader tools (concepts, factors, and experiential truths) that when understood, accepted, and responsibly applied can help make a marriage relationship stronger, more honest, and healthier. *Making marriage work* is what this book is about.

When a man and woman make the decision to enter into a lifelong covenant relationship, three points deserve serious consideration. They are the following: 1) what one brings and puts into this relationship; 2) how one views the unique and special quality of this relationship; and, 3) the effort and discipline one is willing to put into this relationship to keep it going and to keep it growing.

A personal reminiscence from my childhood serves to illustrate the first point. My parents were born in Lancaster County, Pennsylvania and came from rather large families. My mother was one of seven children; my father was one of fifteen children. They were the only two from their respective families that not only moved out of the county but also out of the state! But my parents never forgot or totally left their roots. Growing up, I spent many summers and holidays visiting cousins, aunts, uncles, and grandparents in Lancaster County. One of my favorite relatives was my great-aunt Lulu. She was a large, jolly, and pleasantly boisterous woman who came from Mennonite-Amish stock. She was a widow who owned and operated her own farm. Although she employed two farm hands, she chose to do much of the farm work and daily chores herself.

I loved to visit my great-aunt Lulu, not only because as a New York City boy I got to see real live chickens, ducks, pigs, and milk cows, but especially because she made the very best homemade donuts in the entire world! Aunt Lulu knew I loved her donuts. Every time we made a visit to her farm she would greet us at her front door and loudly proclaim: "Come on in. Whatcha waitin' fer? I got some donuts that just came outa the oven." In we'd go, and there on her huge kitchen table was a tray of the freshest, warmest, and most indescribably delicious donuts that could possibly exist.

I don't know what made my great-aunt Lulu's donuts so good. She said it was in the "makin'." Aunt Lulu must have been right for my mother and three of her sisters copied her recipe for donuts and they tried numerous times to produce the same kind of donut. But they never seemed to make donuts that looked, tasted, or smelled as good as my great-aunt Lulu's donuts. They copied her original recipe. They put in the same ingredients. They followed the same directions. But their donuts *never* looked the same or tasted as good as great-aunt Lulu's donuts.

Why was this so? I believe it was as Aunt Lulu said, it was "in the makin'." The proper ingredients and following the instructions were not enough. There was a certain amount of love, care, concern, and special attention that Aunt Lulu incorporated in the making of her donuts that made them so special and so good. I'm convinced that in terms of country cooking, and especially in making donuts, my great-aunt Lulu was a skilled and creative artist.

The same can be said of a marriage relationship—*it's all in the making!* One may know the recipe, have the right ingredients, and follow the instructions. But if a marriage relationship is to last and withstand the continual stresses and strains (both external and internal), it requires more than a recipe. It needs the love, care, concern, and special attention of the participants. For a marriage relationship to grow and to thrive it takes skill and creative artistry. "It's all in the makin'."

The second point has to do with the uniqueness and special quality of the marriage relationship itself. Webster's New World Dictionary (Third College Edition) defines marriage as a "close or intimate union." Because of its closeness and its intimacy, it is "not to be entered into unadvisedly, but reverently, discreetly, and in the fear of God."[1] It most certainly is a union—a union of body, mind, and spirit. In the biblical creation account of human beings as presented in Genesis, the woman received her name because she was taken out of man: "That is why a man leaves his father and mother and is united with his wife, and they become one" (Genesis 2:24) TEV. If a marriage relationship is to function in a healthy way, it needs to be seen, accepted, and lived as a unique, special and God-given relationship. In fact this book is based on the reality that next to one's personal relationship with God, the marriage relationship is the most intimate, special, and important relationship that a human being can have with another human being. This relationship is crucial because it has an impact on all other human relationships. Today numerous social scientists, mental health professionals, and educational experts (as well as government and civic leaders) see a connection between social problems and family problems. In reality, the connection goes beyond that. For the condition and health of a family is connected to the condition and health of a marriage. In a very real sense it can be said, "So goes marriage, so goes life." The health and vitality of the marriage relationship have implications not only for a person's life in particular but also for life in general.

Making marriage work involves *a third point that must be taken into account.* The creative making of a marriage is certainly an important point. Seeing marriage as a special relationship that has lifelong and life enhancing aspects to it is another. But the third point is as crucial as the other two. *A marriage relationship, particularly if it seeks to be a healthy and strong relationship, requires work—constant work.*

I have been married for 30 years. Throughout those 30 years it has been a wonderful, creative, and dynamic marriage relationship. One can say that I have been fortunate. But the condition and health of my marriage has not been the result of good luck. One can say that I have been blest. But God did not give me and my wife any special consideration over other married couples. God blest our marriage because we worked hard at it and we put Him at the head of it. For us, God was not only the Lord of life, He was and remains the Lord of our relationship! My wife, Betty, and I have worked hard, and labored long, in the prayer, practice, and performance of our marriage. And whenever we started to get lost along the way God would put us back on the right track!

One cannot afford to be lazy and nonchalant concerning marriage unless one cares little about the results. The computer age did not invent the concept of garbage in garbage out. Rather it is a truth that applies to anything in life that is worthwhile and worth having. The old adages of "You get what you pay for" and "Nothing worthwhile in life is free" are particularly true concerning marriage. One works hard to excel in school and in one's career. The conscientious student, athlete, and careerist know that inspiration and skill are not enough. Perspiration, practice, and discipline are required to move ahead and get established in life. In that respect the career of marriage is no different. *It takes work—sweat and tears kind of work!*

In my role as a U.S. Navy chaplain I've had the opportunity to provide premarital workshops and marriage enrichment programs to hundreds of men and women in a variety of settings. In these workshops and enrichment programs, as well as in my counseling sessions with individuals and couples who are married or who plan to marry, I have used a model that encourages participants to take seriously the dynamics involved in making marriage work. This model, when applied and appropriately used, provides persons with a process and a direction in making the relationship of marriage stronger, more honest, and more fulfilling. This model is based on a biblical account of a marriage relationship that existed 2,500 years ago! I call this model the Hosea Model, because it represents a marriage relationship found in one of the books in the Bible—the book of Hosea.

AN OVERVIEW OF THE HOSEA MODEL

An exploration of how the Hosea Model functions as a biblical model for marriage will be addressed in chapter 1. The Bible contains numerous models which provide guidance and insights into the human experience. Abraham, Ruth, and David are just three examples of personages whose biblical narratives can serve as models for human behavior. In particular, the story of Hosea's marriage to Gomer provides a picture of unfailing love in the midst of brokenness. As a biblical model for marriage, it speaks to the importance of commitment, cost, standards, and how the marriage relationship directly affects other kinds of human relationships.

Chapter 2 focuses on the importance of commitment in marriage. In many of today's relationships, there is confusion about what commitment is and what is required in order to have a commitment. How can commitment become a viable and relevant factor in the relationship of marriage? An analysis of some of the basic desires found in the formation of personal relationships between men and women will be discussed. Contrasting desires with commitment will help show why desires alone are not sufficient in providing the substance and foundation necessary to hold a relationship together. Finally, a biblical understanding of commitment as a covenant relationship conveyed in the model of Hosea will be addressed.

In chapter 3 the cost involved in marriage will be explored and discussed. Why is there a price involved in maintaining a relationship? The importance of "giving way" in a relationship will be examined. Consideration will also be given to six important questions that need to be raised and dealt with in the context of marriage. In terms of the Hosea Model, the cost involved in Hosea's marriage played a key role in reconciling a broken relationship between himself and his wife. That cost relevantly speaks to the price required to make marriage work today.

Chapter 4 will take a look at the standard required in a marriage relationship. Why is a standard necessary, and what can it offer to persons within the relationship of marriage? The steps necessary in making the relationship of marriage grow in health and in maturity will be examined. In particular, eight ways to measure a marriage's health will be discussed and shown how to be used as helpful tools for relationship evaluation. In terms of the Hosea Model, the establishment of a standard provides an internal yardstick by which the marriage relationship can be assessed.

Chapter 5 will explore the parallels implied in the relationship of marriage. Is there a connection between the state of one's marriage and the state of many other kinds of relationships in one's life? The conditions affecting the communication process in relation to marriage and its connection to other relationships will also be discussed. From the Hosea Model one discovers that the health and well-being of a marriage relationship can affect the health and well-being of one's relationship to God.

Finding relationship models that work will be the focus of chapter 6. Are there models of persons and their relationships that are worthy of emulation? Can one's own personal relationships serve as models for others? Creating the right atmosphere, establishing specific priorities, and maintaining certain habits will be looked at in terms of making marriage relationships healthier and stronger.

In each chapter of this book a specific truth, as revealed in the Hosea Model, will be explored and critiqued as a guideline for marriage relationships today. Hosea was able to convey how the personal relationship of his marriage relates to God's relationship with God's people. The applications and insights one gains from the Hosea Model can definitely become key ingredients in making marriage work!

CHAPTER ONE:
THE HOSEA MODEL

"I will betroth you to me forever; I will betroth you in righteousness and justice, in love and compassion. I will betroth you in faithfulness, and you will acknowledge the Lord. 'In that day I will respond,' declares the Lord—'I will respond to the skies, and they will respond to the earth; and the earth will respond to the grain, and the new wine and oil, and they will respond to Jezreel. I will plant her for myself in the land; I will show my love to the one called 'Not my loved one.' I will say to those called 'Not my people,' 'You are my people'; and they will say, 'You are my God.'" (Hosea 2:19–23) NIV.

For more than 18 years, I have used the Hosea Model in my marital and premarital counseling ministry with men and women in the military. The Hosea Model has been used with the U.S. Navy, the U.S. Coast Guard and the U.S. Marines. I have used this model at training centers, air stations, naval facilities, family service centers, medical centers, and on board ships. As a therapeutic model, it has worked well in personal counseling with couples and with individuals. And in the format of a seminar or workshop with either small or large groups, it has been evaluated by most participants as both suitable and relevant. It is also a model that has adapted well to both marriage enrichment and marriage preparation classes.

What specifically is the Hosea Model? How does it offer guidance on making marriage work? *First and foremost, it is a biblical model of a marriage relationship grounded in human experience.* It is a model which provides specific truths useful to marriage. When these truths are seriously taken into account and personally applied, marriage relationships grow, prosper, and mature.

A BIBLICAL MODEL

The Bible is God's word in human form. It provides the insights, truths, and guidelines we need to live (and as God would have us live), as mature,

1

responsible, giving, and loving human beings, in healthy relationship with others, self, and God. The Bible offers a vast and varied collection of writings. These writings provide abundant food for the heart, mind and soul. In scripture, numerous narratives reveal what happens when the human character becomes confronted, challenged, and changed by God's intervention and guidance. It is within such biblical narratives one can find models of behavior and action applicable to the problems, issues, and needs of men and women today. Examples of such models are found in the biblical accounts of Abraham, of Ruth, and of David and Bathsheba.

Abraham

Abraham has been referred to as a "wandering Aramaean." He was one who traveled with his family from one town to another seeking the ideal place to live. It was not until Abraham encountered God and was told, "Leave your country, your people, and your father's household and go to the land I will show you" (Genesis 12:1) NIV, that he discovered a mission and a purpose in life worth pursuing. Abraham left his home, his relatives, and his familiar surrounding. He began an adventure which offered and also provided abundant blessings for him and his family. Abraham became the father of a great nation and the spiritual father for millions of believers today.

The narrative of Abraham's journey and encounter with God can provide numerous insights and truths for people looking for a mission and purpose in life today. The story of Abraham serves as a model of faith and of a response to God's call having many contemporary applications.

Ruth

Ruth was an individual who moved to her mother-in-law's hometown with inadequate resources to make it on her own. She had no financial support, no employment opportunity waiting for her, and no guarantee of the necessities of food, clothing, and shelter. In addition, Ruth entered a new community with three strikes against her. She was a woman. She was a widow. And she was a foreigner. Even in the midst of such hardships, Ruth had a love and a loyalty for her mother-in-law that would not quit. Her words to her mother-in-law, Naomi, express that loyalty and love: "Don't urge me to leave you or to turn back from you. Where you go I will go, and where you stay, I will stay. Your people will be my people and your God my God. Where you die I will die, and there I will be buried. May the Lord deal with me, be it ever so severely, if anything but death separates you and me" (Ruth 1:16–17) NIV.

The story of Ruth is a story of perseverance in the midst of great uncertainty. It is a story which becomes a biblical model concerning love and commitment providing a powerful and inspirational testimony for those facing obstacles and difficulties today.

David and Bathsheba

As a middle-aged king, David had it made. Wealth, power, recognition, success—he had it all. Nevertheless, it all came into question on the day he took a stroll around the roof top of his palace, as his army waged another war to increase the size of his kingdom. Gazing down upon the courtyard of one of his officers' quarters, he saw a woman taking a bath. That one look was all it took for him to decide she was someone he must have. David's stroll on his roof top garden led him to the temptation, opportunity, and conscious choice of having an affair with another man's wife.

When the affair resulted in the woman's pregnancy, David sought a way to avoid the responsibility for his actions. Because his plan to blame the woman's pregnancy on her husband's brief return from the war did not work (even a quickly devised backup plan fizzled), a flustered and frustrated David sent the husband back to the front line and to certain death. After the proper time of mourning was over, David had the grieving widow move into his own house. He then married her.

David clearly knew the seriousness of the violation in which he was engaged. He certainly knew the penalty if exposed. But these realities were not on the front burner of his thinking. It took an outsider to these events, the prophet Nathan, to boldly confront the king and expose him to the reality of what he had done. David's lust and greed nearly destroyed him because he chose not to control his desire to have something he knew was wrong for him to have. David paid a price of personal grief for his indiscretion and abandonment of his ethical and moral principals.

After David married the widow Bathsheba, the child born to them soon became very ill. David did everything he could to keep the child alive. He pleaded. He prayed. He fasted. He even shut himself away from others and spent his nights lying prostrate on the ground. A week later, the child died. Scripture reports the following: "David's servants were afraid to tell him that the child was dead, for they thought, 'While the child was still living, we spoke to David but he would not listen to us. How can we tell him the child is dead? He may do something desperate'"(2 Samuel 12:18) NIV.

Nevertheless, David's actual response to his son's death was more disconcerting than desperate. After being bathed, shaved, perfumed, and dressed in fresh, clean clothes, David sat to a sumptuous meal. His servants were puzzled and confused. Had not David acted like someone in great agony? Had he not seemed to be on the verge of a physical and mental breakdown? How then can the king sit, dressed, combed, and in fine clothes, ready to partake in a feast? When asked about his seemingly strange behavior, David had this to say: "While the child was alive, I fasted and wept. I thought, 'Who knows? The Lord may be gracious to me and let the child live.' But now that he is dead why should I fast? Can I bring him back again? I will go to him, but he will not return to me" (2 Samuel 12:22–23) NIV.

The biblical account of David's affair with Bathsheba involves more than a description of an individual's failings and unethical decision-making. Besides speaking to the issues of moral character and the consequences of one's actions, this account also speaks to the need for remorse, repentance, and the importance of knowing when to let go. This particular story provides a biblical model not only for those facing the real dangers of power and success, but also for those wrestling with the need for confession and healing in their work, in their relationships, and in their lives.

Three biblical accounts, each providing insights and guidance for similar human predicaments today. The story of Abraham has much to say to those seeking direction and looking for goals that count in their lives. The story of Ruth speaks to those needing love and seeking human goodness in the midst of personal struggle and difficulty. The story of David and Bathsheba speaks to those who have succumbed to the temptations of lust and the misuse of power and who seek forgiveness, healing, and wholeness in their lives. For those seeking insights and meaning in the relationship of marriage, the Bible offers another model. This model is found in the story of Hosea. It is a model which speaks powerfully and poignantly to the special relationship of marriage.

THE STORY OF HOSEA

The story of Hosea is the story of great personal crisis set in the midst of tremendous national and spiritual crises. Hosea was one of the four great biblical prophets of the 8th century B.C. Although his message was not unique, the delivery of that message through the brokenness of his own marriage relationship certainly was.

Hosea lived in the tiny northern kingdom of Israel, in a time of continual political and social unrest. The two great superpowers of that age, Egypt and Assyria, threatened the existence of the tiny kingdom of Israel. Israel was often caught in the middle of a very dangerous game in attempting to placate one superpower while trying to appease the other. In this little northern kingdom, deceit, corruption, greed, and moral and spiritual decay became everyday occurrences. Widows and orphans were neglected and ignored. Bribery was a frequent practice. Political and religious hypocrisies were the rule rather than the exception. Hosea 4:1b–2 describes the situation this way: "There is no faithfulness, no love, no acknowledgment of God in the land. There is only cursing, lying and murder, stealing and adultery; they break all bounds, and bloodshed follows bloodshed."

Hosea looked at his country and his people and saw nothing but unfaithfulness. There was unfaithfulness in his people meeting human needs. There was unfaithfulness in their relationships with each other. And there was unfaithfulness in his people's relationship with the Lord. Hosea chose to condemn his own people for their behavior. He had nothing but contempt for their lack of faith. He had already judged and sentenced them in his own mind.

In the midst of so many fractured and broken relationships, Hosea had his very own tremendously difficult and strictly personal relationship with which to contend. He married a woman named Gomer who bore him three children. The first child, a son, was given the name Jezreel. Jezreel was also the name of a valley where Israel had suffered a humiliating military defeat. One can only imagine how others viewed such a name. To name a child Jezreel in that day would be like naming one of today's children "The Bay of Pigs" or "America's failure in Vietnam"—not a very popular or socially acceptable thing to do!

Hosea's second child, a daughter, was given the name Lo-Ruhamah—which means "not loved." Through the naming of this child, Hosea was showing his conviction that God should no longer love Israel due to its unrepentant behavior. The third child, another son, was given the name Lo-Ammi—which means "not my people." It was Hosea's belief that the name of this child served to symbolize God's final break with his people. Hosea had come to the conclusion that Israel would no longer be God's people and God would no longer be their God.

The naming of these three children not only served to represent the intolerable conditions Hosea saw around him, it also served notice that as a prophet of God, he had wiped his hands of his neighbors, his people, and his nation. And from Hosea's point of view, *God had done the very same thing!*

Yet, as the Bible so often has the temerity to point out, God's perspective and ways of doing things do not always conform to human perspective and ways of doing things. If it is God's will and desire, God can take a valley of defeat and humiliation named Jezreel and remake it into a place of harvest and abundance. God can take one who is not loved and change him or her into one who *is loved.* God can even take those called "not my people" and transform them into persons who are God's people and into those who recognize and accept God as their God (Hosea 2:21–23).

Hosea may have thrown in the towel concerning any redemption and reconciliation possibilities with his people, but God had not done so! Hosea was about to learn how God could challenge and change the hearts of persons, including his own. This lesson would come through Hosea's own marriage! One day Hosea returned home to discover that his wife had left him. She left him not just for one lover, but for a whole series of lovers. Gomer had become a prostitute—most likely a cultic prostitute in one of the pagan fertility cults prevalent in the society of that day.

When Gomer left him, Hosea faced a dilemma. He had an important decision to make. He could decide to wipe his hands of his unfaithful wife and declare his marriage to be at an end. Yet that was not the choice he made. Instead, Hosea decided to go after his wife, find her, and bring her back. When Hosea found his wife, he literally bought her back from those who owned her. He then made it clear to her that he would take her back as his wife (and not as a piece of property to be bought and sold) on the provision she end her adulterous ways and become faithful sexually and in every other way to him alone.

Why had Gomer left Hosea? The biblical account is silent on this question. Considering Hosea's dim view of his own people and of the society in which he lived, Gomer may have found herself in a relationship with a husband who gave her less than adequate love and emotional support. Was she married to a man without love? A judge without mercy? A husband without forgiveness? How did she feel having her children given such harsh names? How did she react to having her family, friends, and neighbors rebuked and condemned by Hosea? If her husband was her window to God, why would she want to look there? Speculative questions, yes. Nevertheless, they are valid ones to raise if one is open to the view that Hosea's own broken marriage required healing and restoration before Hosea would be able to convey God's message of healing and restoration to a broken people.

The story of Hosea is about revealing sin and unfaithfulness and the consequences that result from doing so. However, it is also a story about love, repentance, and redemption. It is a story that begins with pain and despair and ends with blessing and hope. Hosea's marriage relationship, intentionally or not, had become a symbol of God's relationship with his people. It was a special relationship that dramatically showed, even in the midst of severe brokenness, how it could still be mended, healed, and restored.

HOSEA: A BIBLICAL MODEL FOR MARRIAGE

The account of Hosea's relationship with his wife provides a picture of how unfailing love can prevail even in the midst of unfaithfulness. It also shows how a broken relationship can be restored. The relationship crisis in Hosea's own marriage portrays a biblical model providing relevant truths and insights for marriage relationships today. It is an example of how the human experience of one can relate to the human experience of many. Specifically, the Hosea model points to four important truths concerning marriage.

Truth Number One: A marriage relationship requires a *commitment.*

Truth Number Two: A marriage relationship involves a *cost.*

Truth Number Three: A marriage relationship must have a *standard.*

Truth Number Four: A marriage relationship affects *parallel* relationships.

Commitment

"The Lord said to me, 'Go show your love to your wife again, though she is loved by another and is an adulteress. Love her as the Lord loves the Israelites, though they turn to other gods and love the sacred raisin cakes'" (Hosea 3:1) TEV. Hosea viewed his attempt at reconciliation with his wife as a divine mandate. It was a command from God. Hosea became morally bound to do everything possible to mend a broken relationship with his wife. His commitment to the marriage relationship meant he was ready and willing to pull out all the stops to get his marriage back on the right track.

Regarding the relationship of marriage, the Hosea Model clearly points to the necessity of commitment. *Commitment provides the glue that holds a marriage relationship together.* Without a firm and strong commitment a marriage relationship is no longer special, long-lasting, or secure. Without commitment a relationship too easily becomes tenuous, casual, and temporary. Casual affairs, one night stands, and living together to see what develops are all relationships without commitment. Commitment is necessary and essential in making a marriage relationship work!

Cost

"So I bought her for fifteen shekels of silver and a homer and lethek of barley" (Hosea 3:2). Hosea shelled out fifteen pieces of coin and about ten bushels of grain to buy back his wife from those who now owned her. For Hosea there was a definite cost involved. He got back his wife, but he had to pay a price! God made it clear to Hosea that not only was he to continue to love his wife, he had to go find her and literally buy her back.

The Hosea Model forces one to confront the reality of the cost involved in having a relationship. *There is always a cost involved in reconciling a broken marriage relationship.* Nevertheless, is one willing to pay the price? Making promises, establishing trust, practicing forgiveness, and providing flexibility and adaptability in a marriage relationship are all costly. The risks of being hurt, disappointed, let down, and wronged are not only possible but real. In maintaining a viable marriage relationship the cost is high—*but that is exactly the point!*

Standard

"Then I told her, 'You are to live with me many days, you must not be a prostitute or be intimate with any man, and I will live with you'" (Hosea 3:3). Hosea laid out the ground rules for the continuation of their relationship. Things would not be the same as before. A new set of criteria must be established between them as husband and wife. Hosea made the choice to pay the price of buying back his wife. Now Hosea decided to set up a standard. He told his wife that they would live together as husband and wife but not have a sexual relationship until other matters between them got worked out. Nor was she to resume her adulterous activities with others if the marriage relationship was to continue. By setting a firm standard

Hosea made it possible to have a time for careful reflection and evaluation. It would be a time that allowed for careful consideration and the possibility for positive change in their relationship.

In terms of the Hosea Model, having a standard in a marriage relationship is a requirement, not a recommendation! *A marriage relationship must have some kind of standard if it is to stand.* A standard establishes a measure by which a relationship can be evaluated and tested. A standard in a marriage means that the partners involved already know what the guidelines are. They have clearly communicated to each other what the beliefs, practices, and rules of their particular relationship are and will be. A standard provides the internal yardstick by which a marriage can be assessed.

Parallel

"In just this way the people of Israel will have to live for a long time without kings or leaders, without sacrifices or sacred stone pillars, without idols or images for divination . . . the time will come when the people of Israel will once again turn to the Lord their God. Then they will fear the Lord and receive his good gifts" (Hosea 3:4–5) TEV. Hosea began to see a similarity in his relationship with his wife and his people's relationship with God. "In just this way . . . ," Hosea says. In just this way God will do to the people of Israel what I have done to get back my wife. There was parallel involved in what happened to Hosea and his wife and to what happened to Israel and God. If reconciliation and restoration were possible in the one situation, it was certainly possible in the other.

From the Hosea Model, one recognizes the parallel that exists between a marriage relationship and other relationships. *The health and state of well-being of a marriage relationship are analogous to the state and well-being of other kinds of personal relationships.* Many characteristics found in the relationship of a marriage are similar to those found within other kinds of relationships. When a marriage is in a crisis, it adversely affects how one sees life and one's relationship to it. When a marriage is happy and fulfilling, one's view of life and of other relationships are enhanced. In other words, there is a definite parallel involved.

APPLYING THOSE TRUTHS TODAY

The necessity of making a commitment, taking account of the cost involved, establishing and communicating a specific standard, and seeing the parallel that a marriage relationship has with other relationships, are four truths relating to marriage that are revealed by the Hosea Model. These truths are timeless and relevant. Such truths can appropriately and effectively apply to the evaluation of any marriage relationship. And such truths have much to say concerning the wellness and wholeness needed in many of today's marriage relationships.

The following chapters of this book address the techniques, insights, and examples I have used in applying the truths of the Hosea Model to marriage in my counseling ministry. The Hosea Model is shown to be a relevant and timely model providing guidance and direction for men and women actively seeking to make their marriage relationships healthier and better.

CHAPTER TWO:
THE COMMITMENT NEEDED

"Your Creator will be like a husband to you—the Lord Almighty is his name. The holy God of Israel will save you—he is the ruler of all the world" (Isaiah 54:5) TEV.

"The people who are most convinced that marriage is a failure are those who have tried it most often."[1]

SIGNS OF THE TIMES?

A recent movie made for television dramatized the affair a highly successful architect was having with a professional colleague.[2] He apparently enjoyed a good relationship with his wife and college age daughter. However, he met and fell head over heels in love with another woman who is also an architect. Viewing himself as a considerate human being, he told his wife about the affair. He also told his wife that he still loved her but planned to continue seeing the other woman. When the other woman discovers she has leukemia and would only have three to four months to live, he decides to spend the next few months with her rather than with his wife. During the next couple of months, the wife goes through all kinds of emotional hurt, pain, and suffering. The college age daughter also goes through her own crisis concerning personal relationships. Meanwhile, the man spends every moment he can with his dying girlfriend. No one at home or at work questions or confronts him directly about his choices or his behavior. He freely admits to the turmoil and emotional upheaval he is causing. Nevertheless, he cannot understand or appreciate the hurt and pain others feel—and this is especially so when the hurt and pain emanate from his very own family.

In the 1970s, another television movie entitled *Torn Between Two Lovers*, dramatized a very similar theme. However in that particular movie, it was the wife who was having an affair. A successful and attractive businesswoman (played by Lee Remick) met a successful architect (played by

10

George Peppard) when the plane they were both on became grounded during a snow storm in Chicago. The businesswoman was married to a kind and loving man. She had two intelligent and well mannered teenaged children. Nevertheless, the architect's charm and debonair ways were just too irresistible for her to resist. Thus she became involved in a hot and heavy love affair. The snow eventually melted in Chicago, but the affair did not! The woman chose to continue seeing "the other man" and continue in her marriage and family life as if nothing significant had taken place.

From the woman's perspective, her two lives and her two loves would have continued were it not for three events that threw a monkey wrench into her plans. First, her two children found out about her affair. They bluntly told her, "Mom, what you are doing is wrong and we do not like it." Secondly, her husband discovered what she was. As a result, he packed his bags and moved out of the house. He also gave his wife an ultimatum, "Choose. It is either him or me. You cannot have it both ways." Third, the architect told her that he loved her and wanted to marry her. He did not want just an affair; he wanted a permanent relationship. As the confused and perplexed businesswoman weighed her options, the theme song of the movie (also entitled "Torn Between Two Lovers") played louder and louder on the soundtrack.

What a difference twenty years make! In the 90s version of this tale of infidelity no one confronts or challenges the choices made or the behavior displayed. The architect's coworkers, who clearly saw what was going on, said nothing. The architect's daughter never asked her father how he could do such a thing. Nor did she confront him with how his continued relationship with another woman was hurting both her and her mother. His wife never challenged his choices by saying in effect, "Yes, I am sorry your girlfriend is dying of cancer. *Nevertheless, you are married to me. Your wedding vows were made to me, not her. You can't have us both.* If you choose to move in with her for the next four to six months of her illness then say good-bye to me. There are consequences involved in what you choose to do!"

No challenges. No confrontations. No taking responsibility for the choices made or the consequences received. The television movie ended with the architect returning home after his girlfriend's death and discovering his wife was launching out on a life of her own. So he goes to a restaurant and sits alone wondering why he is unable simply to resume his life and his relationships as they were before.

Moral ambiguity and ethical malaise concerning the marriage relationship were more than just themes. *They clearly were at the heart and soul of this movie!* The power of the movie's message was not in what it said but in what it showed—a view of many people's personal lives today that's clearly on the mark.

In a recent interview, noted author and marriage and family counselor Dr. Gary Rosberg was asked why so many marriages are falling apart and why there is so much pain in personal relationships today. Rosberg pointed out that married couples no longer have a map to help them handle problems. Without clear directions in their lives and in their relationships, people can easily get lost and confused. When specifically asked the question, "What in the world has led us to this current state of marital pain?" Rosberg replied, "Part of it lies in the basic root of selfishness in all of us . . . By nature we are selfish. What is happening to this culture today that is different from 30, 25, 35 years ago is that now all the rules are being thrown out the window . . . You don't have to be committed. You don't have to finish the race with the wife of your youth."[3]

Today there are fewer and weaker boundaries (moral, cultural, social, or institutional) to contain and control selfishness. In the development of relationships, when all the rules and standards are thrown out, marriages and families suffer the consequences. In spite of infidelity and moral ambiguity in marital relationships, commitment can still provide the glue needed to hold those relationships together. But it is essential that such commitment is not based on faulty assumptions.

MAKING COMMITMENT A VIABLE ISSUE

Commitment is not a dead issue today, although it appears that is indeed the case. The problem lies not in its death but in its viability. In the thoughts and plans of many persons who seek to establish a long term relationship, the importance of making a commitment is not a viable priority. Too often, commitment in a relationship is viewed in terms of expectations and desires, and not in terms of responsibility, accountability, and duty. In many modern day relationships, commitment is rarely viewed in terms of a covenant. And God is not even considered or included.

How can we see commitment again as a foundational ingredient in relationships and as a moral obligation that provides needed and firm boundaries for relationships? The answer lies right before our eyes. Reality is a wondrous truth provider. When expectations and desires replace obligation and responsibility, we can clearly see the results.

DESIRE AND EXPECTATION:
SUB-PAR SUBSTITUTES FOR THE REAL THING!

A college football coach was talking to a high school prep star. "Can you run?" he asked.

"Sure can," replied the youth. "Last year I ran two four minute miles." The coach was pleased.

"Can you kick?" asked the coach. "Of course," replied the student. "I've kicked several footballs out of the stadium." The coach began to take notes.

"How about tackling?" said the coach as he put pen to paper. "No problem. Last year I knocked five players out of the game with my tackling," boasted the student. By now the coach was beaming.

"How about grades?" he asked. "Straight A's since kindergarten," came the response. By now the coach was ecstatic.

"Do you have any faults that I should know about?" concluded the coach.

There was a long pause. Finally the student replied, "Just one. I do have a tendency to stretch the truth quite a bit."

Talk is not an adequate substitute for performance. Neither are desires and expectations adequate substitutes for commitment. The neat thing about reality is that it forces us to look at results. What happens to a relationship when anticipation replaces obligation?

When I present workshops on marriage and marriage preparation, I usually begin by handing out a sheet of paper for participants to look at. I ask them to read the contents and informally discuss with one another the material found on the page before the first scheduled presentation begins. The resulting smiles, nudges, chuckles, and whispers taking place between couples and participants tell me that the material they read on that sheet of paper has struck a chord, and perhaps even a nerve, with many of them. This instrument, besides serving as an excellent icebreaker, provides a humorous and often "close to home" view on reality. Read it for yourself.

MARRIAGE VOWS: BEFORE AND AFTER

He married her because among other things, her hair looked so beautiful. He divorced her because she spent so much time fixing her hair.

She married him because his muscles rippled so when he swam. She divorced him because he spent more time in the bedroom doing sitting-up exercises than anything else.

He married her because she was such an adept conversationalist, never at a loss for a word. He divorced her because she never got off the telephone.

She married him because he loved to take her dancing. She divorced him because he was tired most of the time.

He married her because she was so "vivacious." He divorced her because she was too restless.

She married him because he could support her in lavish style. She divorced him because he had too firm a hold on the purse strings.

He married her because their families shared a common background. He divorced her because her family kept interfering in their affairs.

She married him because he had a robust masculine appetite and appreciated her cooking. She divorced him because he never wanted to take her out to eat.

He married her because she was quick, neat, and intelligent. He divorced her because she had absolutely no patience with the children, who were sometimes slow, slovenly, and stupid.

She married him because he was a "real sport." She divorced him because he refused to give up the sporting life.

He married her because they shared the same intellectual and political beliefs. He divorced her because she wasn't interested in anything but the house and the kids.

She married him because he was so courteous and attentive in all the little things, and so oblivious to important things. She divorced him because he was so punctilious about little things, and so oblivious to important things.

He married her because all the other men were so impressed with her magnificent figure. He divorced her, after the third child, because she had "let herself go."[4]

DESIRES AS ELEMENTS IN RELATIONSHIP FORMATION

The biblical insight contained in the words "It is not good for the man to be alone" (Genesis 2:18) NIV, speaks true of human nature. Human beings have a craving for relationships. We become less human when our experiences in human relationships become stunted and distorted. This is certainly the case with individuals who have shown no regard for anyone else but themselves. It is interesting to find in the recent best-selling dual biographical book on the lives of Joseph Stalin and Adolf Hitler, written by Alan Bullock, that the author frequently points to the lack of intimate and well-developed human relationships in the personal lives of both men.[5]

Such insights provide plausible reasons for the insensitivity Stalin and Hitler displayed toward the worth and dignity of human life.

A careful look at the desires most evident in the formation of a marriage relationship can be very helpful. Such study can provide answers to why, in and of themselves, these desires are unable to provide the glue needed to hold a relationship together. In relationship formation, five desires, in particular, come into play. They are the following: the desire for ecstasy; the desire for romance; the desire not to be lonely; the desire for security; the desire to have a family.

THE DESIRE FOR ECSTASY

"He's a dreamboat." "She's a knockout." "Every time I think of him (her), I can't eat or sleep." "That special person puts me on cloud nine, and I've been floating ever since." From the "puppy love" phenomenon experienced as children, to the "hots" phenomenon experienced in the years of youth and adulthood, ecstasy is a sensation that can play havoc with one's senses and one's ability to make responsible judgements. When one falls hook, line, and sinker for someone of the opposite sex, reasoning and logic usually have little or nothing to do with it. In a state of ecstasy (particularly as the cartoonists envision it), the eyes bulge, the heart pounds, the lips drool, and the feet float a few inches off the ground whenever the object of one's desire is encountered or seen.

Ecstasy is a valid and very real condition that occurs as part of one's initial attraction and attention to someone of the opposite sex. It is also a state of bliss that's conditional and temporal. Seeing the "dreamboat" unshaven and disheveled or the "knockout" in face cream and hair curlers more than does the job in deflating the balloon of ecstasy. Ecstasy may have a part to play in one's initial attraction to another person, but it is certainly not the stuff to build a relationship on. A relationship built solely on ecstasy will not cut it. For it can easily float away as quickly as the sensations that triggered it.

THE DESIRE FOR ROMANCE

If romance is understood as experiencing someone else as "ideal" for you and as attributing qualities to that person that you "wish" them to have, then romance can begin to be seen for what it really is—an essentially selfish emotion. The romantic ideal becomes more than just the "perfect person," but the "perfect person for me." I become romantically interested in that person because he or she can provide the key element to my own personality. That "ideal person" can complete the image I have of myself. If I'm tuned into physical attributes, then my romantic ideal must have the perfect body and face. If I'm hooked into the social graces, my romantic ideal is expected to be a great dancer, a lover of the popular arts, and express a gregarious personality. If emotional bonding is all important to me, then the romantic ideal has to be one who is sensitive, caring, and poetically expressive.

More often than not, ecstasy and romance become linked in their power to draw us toward the perfect mate. A little over a decade ago, Bo Derek became the embodiment of the perfect 10. Many young women actively sought to imitate the Bo Derek hairstyle and the Bo Derek look. Males of all ages began rating the attractiveness and sex appeal of females by using a score from 1 to 10. *What many overlooked was that in the movie 10, from which the Bo Derek look and the score sheets on women became the rage, a perfect 10 could still become a complete zero when it came to forming a relationship.* In the movie, Dudley Moore played the part of a man who was driving past a limo containing a bride (Derek) on the way to her wedding. When the man saw the bride from his car window, and realized how beautiful she was, she became the perfect 10 in his mind. She soon became the object of his dreams, his fantasies, and his desires. To say he had been obsessed with her beauty would be putting it mildly. One day, the man's fantasy turned into reality. Because he had personally rescued her from possible drowning, he was presented with an unbelievable reward—an invitation to spend the night in the same room and in the same bed with the perfect woman of his dreams. However, as the soon-to-be rewarded hero got into bed with his perfect 10 prize, something happened. She began to talk! As she talked, the man began to realize that her view of life and interests were very much different from his own. His desire for her ebbed, and he immediately left without his anticipated reward. He returned to his old girlfriend who, in terms of quality of relationship, was the real 10 in his life.

Dr. M. Scott Peck calls the myth of romantic love a dreadful lie.[6] It is a lie because it is not based on reality. It is dreadful because of all the suffering it can cause in the lives and in the relationships of people. A relationship based solely on the romantic ideal will never produce all it promises. Too often, the real payoff becomes not pleasure and fulfillment but pain and emptiness.

THE DESIRE NOT TO BE LONELY

The desire not to be alone is a powerful motivator in relationship formation. In his Journals, the profound Danish thinker, Soren Kierkegaard, spoke of the dread every person encounters when he or she faces the danger of being alone.[7] Kierkegaard's obsession with that dread was a major factor in preventing him from taking the risk of marrying the woman he loved. He was painfully aware of the effect his father's melancholia had on him and he did not want to pass on that kind of pain to the woman he almost married.

Men and women who have served in the military have a special awareness of what it means to feel lonely—this is particularly so for those who have served far away from home or have been on long deployments. My first real taste of loneliness in the military came during my first year as a chaplain on board a ship. It was my first year in the navy and I was assigned to a guided missile cruiser headed to the Western Pacific (WESTPAC) for a seven-month deployment. The timing of the ship's deployment meant that the crew would miss all the major holidays with their families and friends (e.g., Thanksgiving, Christmas, and Easter). In my case, it meant missing the birthdays of my children and my wedding anniversary. During the Christmas holidays our ship made a port call in Hong Kong. Hong Kong was an extremely beautiful city. I had arranged with the navy chaplain stationed in Hong Kong and with the British Counsel to have more than 200 members from our ship spend Christmas day and have Christmas dinner with British families living in various parts of the city. Our crew also held a huge Christmas party on the ship for an entire orphanage of children! Yet with all these things going on, we remained 560 lonely American sailors who were thousands of miles away from our wives, our girlfriends, our families, and our children. We were deeply lonely—so deeply lonely that no activities or festivities with which we were engaged could dispel our deep personal hurt and pain.

The pain of loneliness is real. The dread of that pain is something we as human beings can well identify with. The desire not to be lonely is an element in seeking a bond with someone else. Nevertheless, it will not provide the glue needed to hold a relationship together. It may point to the need for adhesion and proper bonding, but it cannot provide those qualities by itself.

THE DESIRE FOR SECURITY

One of the largest industries in America today is the insurance industry. Insurance has an impact on every man, woman, and child in the USA. As Americans we have our lives insured, as well as our health, our cars, our personal belongings, our homes, and even our loans. Insurance provides security. And everyone wants security! People join labor unions, stay in the military for twenty years, or seek tenure or long-term contracts in their work positions, all because of the security such actions provide. People actively seek financial, physical, and vocational security. Security is the name of the game in our society today.

We also seek emotional security. Being actively involved in a relationship means I do not have to spend time looking for someone else. I don't have to worry about not having anyone to go out with or spend time with. In a relationship, *I've got somebody!* I do not have to put on the mask, play the role, and go to the most popular single place in town trying to pick someone up. Besides, my repertoire of pick up lines may be out of date or seen for what they are—lies to serve myself. In having someone I can count on in a relationship means I don't have to play the dating game anymore—especially if I didn't play it all that well in the first place. The desire for security is an important factor in understanding relationship formation. However, the desire for security alone is not enough to keep a relationship alive and vibrant.

THE DESIRE TO HAVE A FAMILY

As an only child I did not have a brother or a sister to play with when growing up. My father was ten years older than my mother and a variety of work-related injuries had taken their toll on his physical health. My dad knew I loved baseball. One day he picked up a bat and ball and took me out to a field. He wanted to hit the ball to me. I stood out in the field as a twelve-year-old youngster, watching my father grunt in pain as he attempted to hit flies, grounders, and line drives to me. I remember thinking to myself how much I wanted my father to be younger and in better health. Even then, I reflected on how, when I got married and had children, I would make sure that I would be young enough and healthy enough to play ball and enjoy other activities with my own children. Having a family, playing with one's children and getting involved in their activities—all are important experiences. And all provide powerful aspects in the preparation, motivation, and expectation of marriage.

How important such aspects are became clear in my encounter with a particular couple who came to see me because they wanted to get married. In the premarital counseling sessions I had with this couple, I discovered that the respective desires for security and having a family was the compelling issue in their relationship. As a navy chaplain, most people I see who seek to get married are quite young (late teens and early twenties). Nevertheless, this couple was older and appeared more established and settled than many couples with which I do premarital counseling. The woman was in her mid-thirties. She was a nurse who worked in maternity. The man was in his late thirties. He held an executive position in the Boy Scouts of America.

When I agree to do the marriage ceremony for a couple, I make it quite clear that it is a packaged deal. That is, it is a requirement of mine to see the couple for premarital counseling for at least five sessions. These sessions will include such topics as in-laws, pluses and minuses of being married while in the military, finances, communication skills, conflict resolution, and drug, alcohol, and physical abuse. I tell each couple I work with, that it takes at least five sessions to cover as many bases as possible and to prevent either partner from entering into a marriage relationship blind sided. I also explain to them that five sessions of premarital counseling enable them to better understand my investment in their relationship. It is my desire that they see me as a counselor, pastor, and a proponent of healthy relationships, and not as merely a functionary who has the power and license to do wedding ceremonies and sign the proper documents.

This couple not only agreed to the five sessions of premarital counseling; they were extremely enthusiastic in their response. The first two sessions with this couple went extremely well. As an older, more mature couple, both had rewarding occupations and financial security. Both of them owned their own apartments. Their respective families were ecstatic over the news of their impending marriage. (I am sure the fact that they were in their thirties and had never been married added to their parents' excited delight.)

During the third session, I noticed how far apart they sat from each other. I began to realize that I never saw the two of them holding hands or showing any other signs of affection as they entered my office. There were no signs or indications of "lovey-doveyness" in their looks or mannerisms.

So I decided to ask them a direct question: "I have noticed that during the sessions we have spent in this office neither of you has mentioned the word love."

Their response floored me. "Chaplain, we don't love each other!" (It was expressed like, how could I even ask them such a question?)

"If you don't love each other," I asked, "then why do you want to get married?"

The woman replied, "I am a thirty-five-year-old nurse who works in the maternity ward. I see glowing mothers and newborn babies every day. I want to have a baby of my own. I know about Down's Syndrome and about other medical factors that can come into play when one delays child bearing. I want to get married and raise a family before it's too late!"

The man replied, "I'm a Boy Scout Executive. My boss and all my peers at work are married. People wonder why a person my age, and working in the scouting organization, is not married. I don't want others to get the wrong idea. I'm not a playboy, nor am I gay!"

Their blunt honesty and frank responses to my question made it clear what their desires were in getting married. He wanted to get married because of his desire for security in his job. She wanted to get married because of her desire to have a family.

Then I asked them the following question: "What happens after you get married and either one of you, or both of you, discover someone else of the opposite sex who turns you on? What will you do then?"

I saw them for additional counseling. And I suggested that they take some time to be together and see if it were possible for them to become physically and emotionally attracted to one another. I also had them look at some other elements important to consider in relationship formation. Most important, I had them take a close and thorough look at the factor of commitment.

This couple eventually decided to get married. But now it was a decision based on a much more broad and diverse set of reasons than solely the desire to have a family or the desire to have job security.

BACK TO THE BASICS: THE NEED FOR A FOUNDATION

Ecstasy, romance, loneliness, security, and family: each has a part to play in why relationships happen. The validity each has in relationship formation is not in question. I have sought out relationships with the opposite sex in terms of these desires, and so have many others. What is in question is what happens when any one of these desires or combinations of these desires is used to hold a relationship together. Desire alone cannot hold or keep a relationship together. *Desires express needs but they do not provide substance for a relationship!*

Commitment provides substance to a relationship. Desires come from wishes, feelings, and cravings. As longings, desires stem from emotions that are unable to provide the constancy and stability a marriage relationship requires. M. Scott Peck points to commitment as the foundation and bedrock of any genuinely loving relationship.[8] In my view, he's right on! For commitment is the key ingredient in what holds a relationship together.

In the waters of life, too many marriage relationships face tumultuous seas. Is there no anchor available to hold intimate relationships in place amid the unstable conditions that surround them? The biblical account of Hosea's marriage to Gomer (as described in Hosea, chapters 1–3) directs us to one such available anchor—the anchor of commitment.

Hosea's message of God's faithfulness was similar in purpose with the messages of other biblical prophets of the time. What was not similar was the way Hosea chose to convey that message—through the brokenness of his own marriage.

Hosea had married a woman named Gomer who gave birth to three children. Names were given to the children to symbolize the intolerable conditions Hosea saw around him, and to serve notice as God's prophet he had wiped his hands of his neighbors, his people, and his nation. From Hosea's perspective, *God had done no less.*

Hosea may have given up on his people, but Hosea was not God. God could take a place of desolation and transform it into a place of abundance. God could take someone who feels rejected and unloved and have him or her become one who clearly is accepted and loved. God could even take people who are forgotten and forsaken and declare them remembered and redeemed as His own.

Hosea discovered the redemptive power of God through the brokenness of his own marriage. When Hosea discovered that Gomer had left him and what she had become, he had a choice to make. He could declare his wife unfaithful and terminate the marriage, or he could go after his wife and see if reconciliation was at all possible. Hosea made the choice to find his wife and bring her back. Hosea came to see his marriage as more than a contract. It was a commitment involving a covenant relationship with God.

COMMITMENT AS DISPLAYED VIA THE HOSEA MODEL

"Go again and show your love for a woman who is committing adultery with a lover. You must love her just as I still love the people of Israel, even though they turn to other gods . . ." (Hosea 3:1) TEV. Hosea's response to God's word was in the affirmative. He went out seeking to bring back his wayward wife. Hosea did not say to God, "Lord, she's not worth it. How many times must I put up with her infidelity? When my neighbor, Nadab, discovered his wife engaged in a career of cultic prostitution, he publicly divorced her. The entire neighborhood applauded. 'He had every right,' they said. Now that they have recognized my wife as an adulteress, I would be a fool to take her back. Let me wipe my hands of her and get on with my life!"

That conversation is not found in scripture. Nor is it recorded that God said to Hosea, "She's your wife. It's your life. So who am I to mix in? Do what you want, Hosea. It's okay to go with how you feel."

Commitment is not based on wants and feelings. Nor does it rest on what everyone else is doing. Rather a commitment, by its very nature and definition, rests on a promise, a pledge, or a dedication, to a long term course of action. (The oath of allegiance one makes when joining the military, the contract one signs when buying a house or an automobile, the official joining of a club or an organization, all are based on the expectation and assumption that one will fulfill the obligations and responsibilities involved. That is why it is so important in any contract to read *all of it*— including the fine print! One needs to know not only what one is signing his or her name to, but what one is agreeing to. Besides having one's reputation and integrity on the line, there may be financial and legal implications as well.)

When Hosea's wife left, God told Hosea to go and get her back. God said, "Go," and Hosea went. It was a command. It was a command that came from God's covenant relationship with his people, that in God's undying love for his people (even when they are unfaithful) God remains faithful. In the Hosea Model, the anchor of commitment clearly rests on that covenant relationship.

Like the concept of commitment, a covenant can be expressed in terms of a pledge, a promise, or a contract. In the biblical understanding of a covenant the relationship involved is not primarily between two persons but between a person and God. In the biblical understanding of a covenant, God is bound to fulfill his promises. It is in the promise and commands of God that one can find a clear statement of God's purposes and intentions.[9] What makes the covenant relationship far more powerful and necessary than a commitment relationship is that God is in the mix. In fact, God is the essential ingredient!

God's covenant gives structure to our lives. The covenant of God provides reliability and stability in our human relationships and in our moral choice making. In covenant, God's word and God's promise are sure things. God's promises and commands provide security, guidance and fulfillment in the lives and relationships of God's people.[10] But covenant making is not a risk free exercise. There is a definite cost involved. And once the price has been paid a standard must be established to provide guidelines and accountability in marriage.

Paying a price and having a standard are two essential truths also found within the story of Hosea. But these truths have no relevance without commitment. Commitment provides the glue holding a marriage relationship together. Without a strong and secure commitment in marriage, which includes a covenant relationship to God, men and women will find it difficult indeed to keep their marriage relationships special, secure, long-lasting, and life-fulfilling.

I stuck my neck out when I married.
    I knew there would be risks—unknown—a price.
But I was willing to accept the risks along with the
    rewards. And I've been deeply glad.
We stuck our necks out when we decided to have
    a child.
We knew there would be problems, heartaches,
    unforeseeable "costs."
But we were willing, eager to invest ourselves
    in a family.
And we are deeply glad.
    Now this.
You have asked me to accept abundant life.
    All I have to do is surrender my will to thine.
But I'm afraid of the unforeseeable costs.
    Ah, Lord, it's like the rest of my life.
What I really want, I am willing to pay the price for.
    I really want thee.

                        Amen.[1]

SIMILAR CIRCUMSTANCES: DIFFERENT RESULTS

A coast guard cutter went on a three-month deployment. When the cutter returned to its home port, "scuttlebutt" (a sea service term for gossip) soon spread throughout the coast guard family community that some of the cutter's crew had participated in sexual flings while visiting another port. Supposedly, some of the cutter's participants were married men. Two of the wives confronted their home-from-deployment husbands with what they had heard. The two confronted husbands admitted to their infidelity. Both men also made it clear that what they had been involved in was a casual affair—"a one time thing"—and in no way did they want or seek to end their respective marriages.

In less than one week after the ship's return, these two couples came to see me for counseling. The first couple (let's call them A) no sooner sat down in my office when the wife began a verbal assault on her husband. She called him "a jerk," "a weasel," and a few other choice terms much more colorful but also unprintable. The wife then said to her husband, "You dirty scum. You are going to pay for what you did to me. You will never live down what you have done. I'm going to get you back—big time!" And that was just the introduction to her opening remarks!

Less than three days later, the second couple (let's call them B) came into my office. The wife also began the dialogue. Throughout her remarks, she remained calm, although she did appear shaken and emotionally drained. She said to her husband, "You hurt me very much by what you did. I love you and I want to forgive you. But it's very hard. The trust I thought we had as a couple you have taken away. I feel wounded and very much alone."

I often share the information I've just described concerning these two counseling cases with participants in my marriage preparation and enrichment seminars—not only because the two cases were real, were similar, and occurred just a few days apart, but also because they help make a point. After sharing some of the dialogue that occurred in Case A and Case B, I ask seminar participants the following question: In which counseling case do you think reconciliation was possible? Case A or Case B? Seminar responders clearly point to Case B.

In Case A, the upset and enraged wife went for the jugular. Although her husband was in the wrong for what he had done in terms of the infidelity issue, she gave him no time or opportunity to express remorse or to deal in a positive manner with what he had done. In the speed and intensity of her attack, she put him on the defensive. She provided the provocation needed for him to go on the offensive as well. Which is exactly what he did; for he turned to his wife and said, "Who are you to talk to me about infidelity? I've got a list of times and places when you've had affairs of your own!" He then took a list from his wallet and waved it in the air to dramatize his case.

In Case B, the wife was also very upset with what her husband had done. But she chose to share her hurt and pain rather than to focus on her anger. Because she verbalized her hurt and disappointment, she provided an opportunity for her husband to access and question his own actions and what he had done to damage their relationship. He was willing and able to accept her hurt and pain and admit to his own wrong behavior. He accepted his guilt and told her that he was sorry and hoped she eventually would forgive him.

Reconciliation was possible in Case B because the wife was willing to pay a price—the price of her own humanity and vulnerability. By taking the risk of opening up and revealing her own real hurt and pain, she allowed her husband to freely choose what he would do. Would he admit that he was in the wrong and express sorrow and remorse and seek forgiveness? Or would he close the door to the possibility of mending a broken relationship, the rebuilding of trust, and the healing of time?

PAYING THE PRICE OF GIVING WAY

A relationship costs. The ongoing dynamics of a relationship involve bad times as well as good times, sorrows as well as joys, failures as well as successes, and hurts as well as healings. The cost worthy of a mature Christian relationship is described this way in Ephesians 5:21: "Give way to one another in obedience to Christ." The rest of this section in this New Testament Letter (verses 22–33) provides food for thought on what the price of a relationship based in Christ should be. The author of this text goes on to point out that wives are to regard their husbands as they regard the Lord and husbands are to love their wives as Christ loves the church.[2] Throughout this portion of the text, the essential dynamic is to "give way."

"Giving way," is not an easy thing to do in a relationship. In the counseling sessions I had experienced with the two couples who had come to see me for marriage counseling (Cases A and B), on the surface level, their marital conflict appeared to be similar. In both cases, a spouse's affair with a third party had ended. In both cases, it was this affair which had become the revealing issue in a fractured marriage relationship.

Though significantly hurt and emotionally upset, one wife told her husband, that by an act of the will, she still loved him and desired to forgive him—although it would take time to do so. The other wife made it quite clear to her husband that she would never forgive him, and any love for him was out of the question. *In one case, the wife chose to give way.* And because she gave way, marriage counseling, which could help lead to marriage reconciliation and healing, was possible. Because the wife chose to give way, the husband was provided an avenue to give way to his guilt and his pain. A price had to be paid in order for both the husband and wife to give way. But when both chose to do so, it helped them to reestablish their relationship and provide the opportunity for healing. In the other counseling case, the wife made the clear choice not to give way. She wanted her husband to suffer and be penalized *by her* for what he had done. She did not want reconciliation or a relationship restoration. *She wanted revenge!* Give way? Ha! She did not intend to budge an inch. And because that price would not be paid, marriage counseling, the kind which would lead to any semblance of reconciliation and healing, became an impossible task.

When we seriously consider our marriage relationship, what kinds of things should we be giving way to? There are particular questions and related issues which can help us in this task.

SIX QUESTIONS TO ASK IN A MARRIAGE RELATIONSHIP

In the marriage workshops and pastoral counseling I do with couples, participants are provided with specific homework assignments. These assignments incorporate specific tools useful for critiquing and strengthening marriage relationships. One assignment focuses on six questions to ask in a marriage. These six questions were not put together merely to serve as ice breakers or discussion starters. They provide a much more important task. The purpose and intent behind each question is to focus on a significant relationship issue. In responding to these six questions, participants have a better understanding of the cost involved in a relationship. The six questions are the following:

1. What degree of freedom do you have in your marriage?

2. How do you see yourself (in terms of who you are) in your marriage?

3. How much do you understand the other person in your marriage?

4. How flexible are you within your marriage (in terms of crisis, past mistakes, hurts, etc.)?

5. How creative are you within your marriage? (Do you try new ways or go in new directions?)

6. What degree of trust is there in your marriage (in terms of yourself and of your spouse)?

The Issue of Freedom

"What degree of freedom do you have in your marriage?" is an insightful question to ask. Often an issue in marriage is not just the degree of freedom one has but also how one defines and understands freedom. Does freedom within the context of marriage mean one can do as one pleases? What degree and kinds of accountability and responsibility does one marriage partner have to and for the other? Are freedom and marriage two mutually exclusive terms? Or can they work and weave together in positive and creative ways?

It has been my experience that those who have answered the question concerning the degree of freedom in marriage by saying, "I have no freedom"; "I feel boxed in"; "I'm like a prisoner in this relationship"; are clearly unhappy. But so are those who respond by complaining, "I have too much freedom. My marriage partner doesn't seem to care what I do!"

In a relationship, the degree of freedom each partner has is a significant issue. As such, the issue of freedom needs to be defined *by both members* of the relationship. Each member of a marriage relationship needs to know not only where he or she stands on this issue but also where his or her partner stands. The issue of freedom, in terms of a relationship, must also include some aspect of accountability and responsibility. It is important for couples to know that the price of freedom in a relationship does not come cheap!

The Issue of Identity

"How do you see yourself (in terms of who you are) in your marriage?" This question focuses on the issue of one's personal identity within marriage. The issue of identity in a marriage is not to be confused with the function of role. In a marriage, role responsibilities can include such functions as homemaker, bread winner, financial accountant, disciplinarian, educator, etc. The issue of identity has to do with seeing yourself in terms of who you are as a person—as a person who has goals, dreams, and a purpose in life.

Does one's marriage relationship serve to enhance and clarify one's view of self? Or does one's marriage serve to confuse and cloud one's personal identity? "Sometimes I don't know who I am or where I am going in this marriage." "My marriage has helped me grow as a person and have a better understanding of myself." Statements such as these say a great deal about how one sees one's self in the context of marriage.

Those who study the human species have come to the realization that the issue of identity is not resolved at the end of adolescence, or after one's graduation from college, or when one attains a full time career. Rather, the issue of identity remains a valid issue throughout one's adult life, and particularly so as one moves from one transition in life to another. The quality and substance of one's marriage relationship have significant bearing on the clarity and enhancement of one's identity as a person.

The Issue of Sympathetic Awareness

"How much do you understand the other person in your marriage?" is a question involving both communication and sympathetic awareness. "We don't talk anymore!" "I just don't understand him!" "I haven't a clue where she is coming from!" Such comments as these indicate a communication breakdown, particularly on the feeling level.

When I ask couples what they think the biggest problem in a marriage relationship is, the response most frequently given is "communication." (Finance is a close second.) But when couples say that communication is, or can be, a problem in their marriage, what do they mean?

From a relationship point of view, communication means much more than the exchanging of information, the expression of ideas, or the giving and receiving of facts. In terms of a relationship, communication primarily has to do with the sharing of personal feelings. To share feelings in a relationship, an atmosphere of caring, concern, sensitivity, and understanding is needed. If an individual believes his or her personal feelings will be rejected, ignored, demeaned, or attacked, real communication in that relationship will come to an abrupt halt. In terms of a relationship, sympathetic awareness is not just "nice to have," it is a necessary requirement! For one to honestly say, "I try to understand my partner in this marriage," requires being receptive and empathetic of the partner's feelings. If the feeling level is left out of the marriage, so is the communication.

The Issue of Flexibility

"How flexible are you within your marriage (in terms of crisis, past mistakes, hurts, etc)?" is a question which focuses on the resiliency factor within marriage. Persons can bring a lot of emotional baggage to their relationships. In terms of personal relationships, no one has lived in a complete social vacuum. Each of us has experienced hurts, pains, and disappointments, as children, as siblings, as adolescents, and as adults. Each of us has had to face difficulties and disappointments, in our families, in our classes, in our work, and in our daily relationships. The fact that we have encountered numerous emotional upheavals in life is not at issue. But how we have been affected by such unsettling changes is at issue!

Why is it that two married couples can go through similar crises (such as the death of a parent or a child) and experience such different results regarding the resiliency of their marriages? One couple comes through their difficulty with a stronger marriage bond. They are like tempered steel going through the test of fire. The other couple comes through their troubled time with a weaker and more tenuous marriage relationship. The crisis they faced has caused fissures and cracks to take place within the bond of their marriage.

Have previous problems and pains in life served to strengthen and purify our resolve, or have such difficulties worked to weaken and contaminate it? How do we deal with the ups and downs of a relationship now? Do our responses tend to be rigid or flexible? People who hurt from present events and also from past events have difficulty being flexible. Healing people are those who experience healing from present events and have already healed from past events. Healing people are persons in relationships who experience far less difficulty being flexible than persons in relationships who have not experienced healing in their lives.

The Issue of Creativity

"How creative are you within your marriage?" is a question that focuses on the aliveness factor within marriage. When someone calls his or her marriage "stale," "dull," or "boring," creativity and inventiveness are no longer experienced as realities in that relationship.

In a quote attributed to Alex Osborn, it is said: "Creativity is so delicate a flower that praise tends to make it bloom, while discouragement often nips it in the bud." This certainly is the case in the relationship of marriage. In the fast-paced, schedule demanding, time eating world in which so many married people find themselves, the need for creativity in a relationship is crucial. The resourceful and responsible management of time, of important events and celebrations, of schedules, of rest, and of recreational play requires both creativity and sensitivity. Words of appreciation and encouragement, affectionate greetings, and stressing the importance of family celebrations not only serve to undergird a marriage but also helps keep it creative!

The issue of creativity involves the openness one has to the opportunities available in one's life. It involves an understanding of the importance of making choices and examining various options. It involves consideration, kindness and ample doses of praise. It incorporates the on-going challenge of shaping life creatively. And as the following chapter points out, creativity is one of the important dimensions needed in maintaining a healthy marriage relationship.

The Issue of Trust

"What degree of trust is there in your marriage (in terms of yourself and of your spouse)?" This is a two-fold question because the degree of trust that exists in a marriage relationship is a two-fold issue. For example, during the day my wife and I have separate jobs, separate responsibilities and obligations, and separate business and social commitments. I trust my wife when she is working with other men and when she goes to various business meetings and luncheons with persons I may not personally know. I also trust myself when participating in similar functions and activities at my job. I trust myself in knowing when to avoid situations and places that could or would serve to compromise my marriage commitment or cause emotional hurt or distrust on the part of my spouse. In the marriage relationship we have, there is confidence in knowing my wife follows similar guidelines. The trust level in our marriage is high because we both believe in and practice a commitment to marriage involving certain expectations and responsibilities. We have found that open communication, honesty, fidelity, and conflict resolution provide a healthy and mutually satisfactory trust level in our marriage.

This is why the degree of trust in marriage needs to be understood as a two-fold issue. Not only is the question of one's trust and confidence in one's partner an important issue, so is the question of trust and confidence in oneself. How well, and to what extent, do you trust your partner when he or she is in other places and other situations involving other people? How well, and to what extent, do you trust yourself in similar circumstances? The responses given to these kinds of questions provide one of the clearest indicators a counselor has in sensing the wellness and stability of a marriage relationship.

Without an adequate sense of confidence in the truthfulness and trustworthiness of another in a relationship, that relationship faces a rocky road and an uncertain future. When seeing couples for marriage counseling, it is my custom to ask them three very important questions: 1) Has there been any sexual or physical abuse in your marriage? 2) Has there been any drug or alcohol abuse in your marriage? and 3) Is infidelity a present concern in your marriage? These particular questions need to be asked because they deal with very serious issues and dynamics that cannot be ignored, denied, or left out of the process of responsible and accountable marriage counseling. Such concerns set the tone for the kinds of therapy, changes, and healing that are necessary before other aspects of the marriage relationship can be assessed. Abuse and infidelity issues also go to the heart of the issue of trust. Such concerns dissect, open, and lay bare the heart of trust and the condition of its importance and validity within a marriage relationship. Once the bond of trust in marriage has been broken the partners involved need to know it will take time, hard work, and consistency to restore the trust level to what it once was.

RISKS AND REWARDS

Taking a risk in forming and establishing a relationship is most certainly serious business. But it is a *worthwhile business*! There's continual challenge and uncertainty involved when two people come together to form the bond of marriage. As a relationship, marriage is not a past event; rather, it dwells in the present and focuses on the future. This is what makes it a dynamic and ever changing reality. Its importance and relevance as a relationship is evident on the effect it has on other relationships. It is this truth which is the subject and content of the material discussed in chapter 5 of this book.

In the reality of the relationship of marriage, one can experience sorrow as well as joy, pain as well as comfort, and woundedness as well as healing. The willingness to accept such risks as well as rewards involves paying a price. In terms of marriage, the Hosea Model confronts us with what that price may be.

THE COST INVOLVED IN THE HOSEA MODEL

When the prophet Hosea made the decision to wander the streets looking for his wayward wife, he already had some idea of the price involved. To actively seek out one who has wronged you, hurt you, and caused you deep emotional pain, takes a special kind of grit. When one's ego, pride, and sense of righteousness (as in, "I'm clearly in the right here. You're the one who's in the wrong!") take a back seat to restoring a broken relationship, it takes a special kind of courage to make it happen. The determination, perseverance, and stubborn courage required in such a course of action come with a costly price tag.

When Hosea found his wife, she had already become the property of someone else. He had to pay a specific price to get her back. According to Hosea 3:2, the purchase price was "fifteen shekels of silver and about a homer and a lethek of barley." The fifteen shekels of silver Hosea shelled out, as well as the grain he provided, were not by any means a trifle amount. *This was a significant purchase!* Clearly, a transaction of important value had taken place.

This business of relationship mending was costly. Not only did Hosea have to shuck out a chunk of change to get back his wife, he also had to swallow his pride concerning the indignation of being wronged. The cost to do so did not come cheap! By agreeing to take back his wife, Hosea chose to pay the price of giving way. Hosea gave way when he chose to not stop loving his wayward wife. He gave way when he made the decision to pay the price of buying her back. If a relationship is to be reestablished after a difficulty, and if healing is to take place after a time of hurt and pain, then like Hosea, we too must give way to one another in obedience to the Lord.

If the old adage "Nothing worthwhile in life is free" rings true in human experience, then the cost of maintaining a relationship is especially significant. The Hosea Model clearly shows that commitment and cost are two defining truths in a marriage. But they are not the only ones. There is a standard required in marriage as well. It is this third truth which is the focus of the next chapter.

CHAPTER FOUR:
THE STANDARD REQUIRED

"For a Happy Marriage: Ensure that the husband is deaf and that the wife is blind."[1]

"It is my fervent belief that in most cases, the secret to emotional health is to understand that bad things like divorce don't just happen to us, but that in fact we participate in them. In divorce, for example, the sudden exodus of one spouse is usually preceded by years of unmet needs, miscommunication and lack of communication about critical issues."[2]

UNEXPECTED EXPLOSIONS

The first fifteen minutes of the movie *Kramer vs. Kramer* set the tone and atmosphere for the emotional crisis that was to make the dramatization of this film so powerful. When Mrs. Kramer (Meryl Streep) left Mr. Kramer (Dustin Hoffman) suddenly and without warning, she walked out of the marriage and out of her role as parent and mother. Mr. Kramer was left alone to care for their son. He had to become both father and mother to a child he lived with but had not really bonded with. From Mr. Kramer's perspective, he had no idea why his wife suddenly and abruptly left him. To him, everything seemed fine; and his life was orderly and set. There were no serious difficulties, crises, or problems in their marriage that he was aware of. So why would Mrs. Kramer leave him? And more incredulously, why would she abandon her child? However, the film viewer saw the relationship between the Kramers from a different perspective. When Mrs. Kramer chose to leave, her decision was not totally unbelievable to the movie viewer.

During an assignment overseas, I remember an encounter I had with a young man. He spent considerable time walking back and forth in the passage way outside my office. Occasionally he would stop by the front door and peer into the office. Noticing the young man's actions, I walked out of my office and called to him as he continued to pace up and down the deck.

"Want to come in and talk with me?" I asked.

"Sure, Chaplain," he replied. "I've got a slight problem that perhaps you can help me with."

When he took a seat in my office, I asked him what his slight problem was. He told me that he was returning stateside to get married—a prospect that he was very pleased about.

"I'm really excited about getting married," he said. "But the slight problem I am having has to do with the fact that I can't stand my fiancee's parents."

"Why can't you stand her parents?" I asked. (This was more than a *slight* problem!)

"They're of a different religion," he replied.

"If they are of a different religion, then isn't your fiancee also of that religion?"

"Well, that's different. I love her. But I can't stand them!"

As this young man poured out his feelings, I began to learn about his background. His parents were from Northern Ireland. They were both staunch Protestants who had decidedly negative views concerning Roman Catholics. And yes, you guessed it. The young man's fiancee was Roman Catholic.

"Haven't you ever spoken to your fiancee about your family's background and your feelings about Catholics?" I asked.

"Are you kidding?" he cried out. "I'm looking forward to this wedding. I can't tell her that!"

But I wasn't kidding. I was serious. Here was a ticking time bomb primed and ready to blow. One can only imagine the size and impact of the explosion that would erupt when his soon-to-be wife discovered the truth concerning his background and how he and his family felt about those of the Roman Catholic faith. Because principles, values, and beliefs were not established, set down and expressed with his fiancee, this young man's relationship lacked set standards. Without set standards, I seriously wondered how long and how well his marriage would stand.

THE STANDARD FACTOR IN THE HOSEA MODEL

When Hosea brought his wife back from those who owned her, he made it clear that his relationship with her would not mean a return to the old ways of doing things. Conditions had changed in the marriage. It was no longer acceptable doing the same old things. A prescribed time would be set concerning sexual conduct. During this time Gomer would not continue as a prostitute or be involved in adulterous behavior (Hosea 3:3). During this time Gomer and Hosea would live together as husband and wife, but under a different arrangement than before. It would be a time of testing and a time of evaluation—a time specifically set up to see if their marriage relationship could truly be restored and reconciled.

In effect Hosea was saying to his wife, "Gomer, right now we don't have a true relationship. Major changes need to be made. You can no longer be unfaithful to me if you are to remain as my wife. You may agree to our living together. And I may agree to our living together. The reality is time will tell whether this is really possible. If you sincerely want to be faithful to me and you no longer want to continue your wayward ways, then the best proof you can provide rests in not what you say but in what you do. Time will tell in terms of what you intend or don't intend to do. The test of time will be the best evaluator of our relationship."

PREPARING THE GROUNDWORK FOR THE LAYING OF A FOUNDATION

The parables of Jesus have powerful implications and life-enhancing lessons for those who pay heed to the messages presented. That's as true for listeners today as it was for listeners of almost two thousand years ago. The implications and truths expressed in Jesus' teaching concerning the wise and foolish house builders have much to say on people's need for standards.

Apply this parable to the marriage relationship. The wise man who built his home (marriage) upon a rock had a home (marriage) that withstood winds, rain, and flood. But the foolish man who built his house (marriage) upon sand discovered that he no longer had a dwelling (relationship) once catastrophe struck. "The rain came down, the streams rose, and the winds blew and beat against that house and it fell with a great crash" (Matthew 7:27) NIV.

Standards, when well thought out, expressed and established provide the necessary parameters and place in which the foundation of a marriage rests. Establishing such standards in a marriage means the participants are ready and willing to talk to each other about their respective values, principles, and convictions. It is also understood that their intention is to hold on to them in the face of life's difficulties and perplexities. When such standards are established in a marriage relationship, then each participant is able to say, "This is who I am, what I stand for, what I hold to be important, and what I will or will not do in a particular situation."

A standard provides the proper haven in which a marriage relationship rests. If it is a very secure fit, the rock (foundation) cannot be easily rolled away or pushed off a perilous precipice. Knowing and evaluating the multi-dimensional aspects of a healthy marriage is an excellent way to properly prepare groundwork and firmly establish standards.

EIGHT DIMENSIONS OF A HEALTHY MARRIAGE

A second homework assignment that I give to persons involved in premarital and in marital counseling focuses on what is needed to lay the groundwork for a healthy marriage. In particular, the assignment keys in to an understanding and evaluation of eight specific marital dimensions. To prepare participants for this assignment, I first ask them a question. The question is this: *Do you want to make a marriage?* An affirmative response requires a willingness to work hard to make it grow. The shovel and sweat exertion needed in making a marriage grow involves five important steps:

1. Developing a sense of concern (caring).
2. Learning to listen (touching and sharing).
3. Beginning to speak straight (telling the truth).
4. Making a contract (commitment).
5. Working on the dimensions of marriage (eight dimensions).

1. *Developing a sense of concern:* One's willingness and desire to *develop* a sense of concern is of key importance. Caring and concern in a marriage relationship is not a given. Just because two persons enter a marriage relationship with an initial and intense degree of concern for one another is no guarantee that expression of concern will remain constant or consistent. Unless couples vigorously strive to make caring for each other a high priority in their relationship, that kind of caring can take a nose dive and even shrivel up and die.

Concern becomes the chief motivator behind the homework assignments I regularly give to couples who contract with me for premarriage and marriage counseling. In the very first session with them I tell them that they are required to do four different homework assignments that focus on their relationship. Their willingness and effort to participate in these assignments show their level of concern, not only in terms of their relationship but also in terms of each other as persons.

2. *Learning to listen:* Talking to one another is not enough. Distractions, obstructions, and competing interests can play havoc with one's ability to listen and appropriately respond in a marriage. Partners in a marriage say they listen to each other. But do they really hear? Why is it possible for a couple on a beach to hold hands, look into each other's eyes, and communicate without one word being spoken? Could it be that physical touching (physical intimacy) and openness to the sharing of each other's feelings (verbal intimacy) makes such a question mute?

3. *Beginning to speak straight:* "Love rejoices in the truth, but not in evil. Love is always supportive, loyal, helpful, and trusting" (I Corinthians 13:6-7) CEV. These words of the apostle Paul, written to the Christian community in Corinth, speaks volumes about relationship formation. Honesty and truth are essential if a relationship seeks to be secure and established in a mutual bond of trust.

In the homework assignments I give to couples I make it clear that any personal insights and benefits they may gain from the tools shared in the assignments are directly proportional to the honesty and truthfulness of their responses. In other words, the more candid they are in their assessments of themselves and the more honest and truthful they are in their sharing times with each other, the more they will learn and grow in the process.

4. *Making a contract.* When a couple makes a contract with each other they are establishing terms of an agreement. Such terms are clear, concise, and mutually acceptable. Such a contract provides a couple with direction and guidelines. The contract gives credence to their desire for support, encouragement, guidance, and boundaries. Without this anchor of commitment a relationship can lose its mooring. Without a well-defined and established contract, how well will a relationship withstand the stresses and strains of loneliness, boredom, grief, fear, anger, isolation, discouragement, uncertainty, anxiety, and the feeling of being overwhelmed? A contract provides the assurance that the one will be there for the other and vice versa.

When I first see a couple for marital or premarital counseling, I tell them that a contract is required between myself and them. In this contract I agree to counsel them for at least five sessions. At each session I will spend at least 45 minutes with them. At each of the first four sessions I will give them a homework assignment. They are expected to have completed and discussed the assignment with each other before returning to see me. At the end of the five sessions I will look at where they are and where they want to be in terms of their relationship. Such a contractual agreement between them and myself helps to reinforce the reality that I am willing to give them my time, my help, and my commitment in their relationship evaluation and growth. Such an agreement lets them know that I am serious and mean business in working with them. It also lets them know that they are expected to be serious and mean business in their counseling work with me and in their relationship work with each other.

5. *Working on the dimensions of marriage.* In terms of marital growth, the fifth step may be last but it certainly is not least! It is a step that requires the extensive use of the other four steps to effectively work through the various dimensions of marriage.

Marriage, if it is to be vibrant, healthy, and alive cannot be a one-dimensional reality. If it seeks to recognize and accept the active involvement of its participants, it has to be multi-dimensional. Looking at the marriage relationship from a multi-dimensional point of view requires an understanding of those dimensions and the part each participant plays in each dimension. I have couples look at eight specific dimensions necessary for a healthy relationship. They are the following:

1. The Emotional Dimension
2. The Creative Dimension
3. The Social Dimension

4. The Intellectual Dimension

5. The Sexual Dimension

6. The Religious Dimension

7. The Covenantal Dimension

8. The Legal Dimension

1. *The Emotional Dimension*: The very word "dimension" connotes some kind of measurement. In terms of marriage, the extent, degree, and scope of each dimensional quality need to be recognized and carefully evaluated.

As an emotional being, one has a self-interest in what goes on in one's mind and heart. What one personally thinks and feels in a relationship is an important indicator of where one is in that relationship. And that's only one side of the coin. To properly measure the emotional dimension of a relationship one needs to know where the other person is and where that particular person is coming from. How aware are you of what the other member in your relationship is thinking and feeling? To what extent is this information verbalized and talked about?

2. *The Creative Dimension*: This is a measurement of the extent and importance of working and sharing as a team in a variety of areas. In what ways is this relationship a team effort? Why do couples who do work projects together, put up wall paper together, plan vacations together, and make family decisions together seem to handle problems and stress better than couples who each "do their own thing"? Is it possible that teamwork and a personal sense of contributing to a mutual effort provide specific pluses and benefits for a marriage relationship?

3. *The Social Dimension*: I believe it was Charlie Shedd, the noted Christian marriage and family counselor, who once said that dates do not end with marriage. Unfortunately, some married couples don't realize that, particularly when they tend to socially do less together the longer they are married. Many of these same people then wonder why all the sparkle, pizazz, and fun they once had in their marriage are no longer there.

The social dimension includes more than an occasional dinner out, going to a movie, or attending a party. It is an indicator measuring a couple's sharing in recreation and play. Couples who regularly ride bicycles, walk, camp out, play and watch sports, or go on vacations together know what it means to share in recreation and play. They know what it means to laugh, have fun, and to experience special memories and moments together. For such persons, life in general and their relationships in particular are rarely seen in terms of boredom, dullness, or decay.

4. *The Intellectual Dimension*: We live in a world filled with problems, concerns, conflicts, and issues. Events and decisions take place daily that have international, national, local, and personal significance. As human beings, we have opinions, view points, thoughts, and beliefs concerning

these matters. The question is to what extent and how often do we share these concerns and ideas with our spouses?

In marriage counseling, when a person tells me that he or she can no longer talk to his or her spouse, it often follows the following pattern of discourse:

"My husband (wife) never talks to me!"

"You *never* talk?"

"Oh, we talk, but never about anything important. Recently at work I've met this very sensitive and caring man (woman) who really listens to what I have to say. He (she) even asks me what I think about so and so. He (she) actually cares about what I think and what my feelings are on just about everything!"

When a married individual makes comments like these it is a clear indication that sharing in the world of ideas is a dimensional aspect severely stunted or lacking in this person's marriage relationship. It also should serve to wave a red flag in front of the counselor that this apparently platonic relationship with a co-worker may develop (if it hasn't already) into something else.

5. *The Sexual Dimension*: Sex is much more than just a physical act for humans. The mating season may be a reality for many animals but not for the two-legged, walking erect kind. For humans, sex is not a seasonal thing! Fulfillment in this dimension requires *meeting both one's physical and emotional needs.*

We have two cats as pets in our home. Merlin, a thirteen-year-old Persian, was fixed a long time ago and mating is no longer a possibility or of interest to him. Lots of food and sleep are the two major priorities in his life. He seems to care for little else. Carolina is a one-year-old Himalayan. She has been in heat a couple of times. Her sounds and actions make it unpleasant for my wife and me, and also for Merlin who seeks only food and sleep. My wife and I want Carolina to have kittens. So we put up with her noises while we make plans to provide her with a suitable mate.

Unlike cats, the sexual dimension for humans is an ongoing process. It is a dimension that involves one's heart and mind as well as one's body. It is a facet that accepts and expresses a blending of sexual satisfaction and emotional fulfillment. As John L. Thomas, S.J. points out in his classic work on marriage preparation: "Sex is not only something we do; *sex is something we are.* Sex is mind and body, spirit and emotion . . . Because of our sexuality, we have the potential to create love or to destroy it."[3]

6. *The Religious Dimension*: In a relationship, this dimension incorporates much more than what one's religious affiliation is, how often one attends worship services, or whether one is an active member of a particular faith group. The real focus in this dimension is on the degree of willingness and openness in sharing the meaning of life with one's partner. Does your

spouse know if you believe in God? And if so, what kind of God? How do you view life, death, and the question of suffering? Do you believe that your life has a purpose? Do you believe in life after death? In heaven and hell?

There are certain events in our lives that have religious and spiritual significance—death of a loved one, serious illness of a family member, sudden loss of financial resources or material possessions. How are such circumstances in our lives understood, interpreted, and accepted? How are they viewed by our spouse? Is there ever a place in our marital communication for religious dialogue? Or do such events reveal a religious vacuum in our relationship?

7. *The Covenantal Dimension*: This dimension focuses on how well people in a marriage relationship share and stand together in the face of crisis and conflict. Problems, difficulties, and tragedies occur in married life. It is such events as these that often reveal how well a marriage relationship bonds and comes together.

A pastor acquaintance of mine recently discovered she had cancer. Through her ordeal, testing, surgery and prognosis (amazingly good!), her husband was her strongest confidant, supporter, and friend. In a church newsletter, she writes: "I have personally known other men and women who have faced similar dilemmas and as a result painfully discovering their spouse was not there for them in their time of greatest need . . . Finally, I want to say that my husband Frank has been the greatest possible support as he has prayed for me and given care. We cherish each other even more than before."[4]

Cement, when improperly mixed or not given adequate time to properly set, will not hold up under shifting weight and pressure. So too with a marriage relationship that has not been well set, prepared, or bonded. The weight and pressure of life will tear it apart or at the least set it adrift. Why do some marriages go through a variety of crises and personal tragedies and yet come out stronger and more loving than before? Why do other marriages, facing similar difficulties, crack, crumble, and cave in?

8. *The Legal Dimension*: A marriage license is a legal document from the state. It is a written contract between the persons getting married and the state signifying not only a legal marriage but also legal responsibility for specific items and concerns.

HOMEWORK ASSIGNMENTS THAT PRODUCE RESULTS

In my counseling ministry with couples and in many marriage workshops I have conducted, it is a practice of mine to hand each person a piece of paper with a brief description of the eight dimensions discussed in this chapter. I ask each person to take this paper home and spend forty-five minutes to an hour going through a personal evaluation of each of the eight dimensions. The point of reference for each dimension is one's relationship with his or her partner. This evaluation is done by grading oneself in terms of each dimension on a score from one to ten (one being the lowest score and ten being the highest). After grading one's self on how well one is doing in each dimension, the individual then writes down the reason or reasons for the score received. Instructions are given that one grades only one's self and not one's partner. One is an evaluator only on one's self, and the grading is done accordingly.

Once the couple individually completes the assignment, they are required to put aside a *special time* to talk and share their individual assessments with each other. This special time has to be a time of quiet (free of telephone calls, TV shows, or other interruptions). It has to be a time when neither of the couple is overly tired, stressed out, nor emotionally on edge. Each individual shares the score on a particular dimension with one's partner and why a specific score was given. Following this time of evaluation sharing, the couple continues with a dialogue on any questions, concerns, and issues raised as a result.

From the response I have received from the hundreds of persons who have completed this homework assignment, the following assessments can appropriately be made:

High-scoring dimensions reveal specific strengths in a relationship. Couples concurrently scoring eights, nines, and tens in a certain dimension can view this aspect of their relationship as a strength and as an area that does not require a great deal of attention or immediate concern. For example, a couple who has high scores in the creative or social dimension can affirm those strengths while moving on to focus in on another dimension that may require further work and development.

Low-scoring dimensions reveal specific weaknesses in a relationship. Couples both scoring ones, twos, and threes in a specific dimension can see this aspect of their relationship as a weakness which will need concerted effort to strengthen and to develop.

Diversity in the scoring of a dimension (one person scores it high and the other scores it low) reveals the need for further dialogue. In a situation where a particular dimension receives a high score by one person and a low score by the other, the problem can be one of content, or communication, or both. In such circumstances further dialogue is required for the couple to better understand what is going on. Sometimes the situation is such that the couple should seek the assistance and insights provided in marriage counseling to help resolve the issue.

A marriage relationship is multi-dimensional. The time and effort involved in completing this homework assignment enable couples to better understand and appreciate the multi-dimensional aspects of a relationship. This process helps them to see that a marriage based on just one or a few dimensions is stilted and far less fulfilling than one that recognizes and makes use of a variety of dimensions.

WHY A STANDARD IN MARRIAGE IS NECESSARY

When the Prophet Hosea laid out the ground rules for the continuation of his marriage with Gomer, he did so with the hope and possibility for positive changes in their relationship. The standard he established made it possible for the quality of his marriage to be measured and assessed. When couples are fully aware of, and practice, the multi-dimensional aspects of their marriage relationships, they are continually reflecting, assessing, measuring, and evaluating the quality and maturity of those relationships.

Unfortunately, many marriages lack the measuring tools needed to evaluate their health and well-being. Unless couples start communicating to one another what the guidelines and parameters of their particular relationship will be, the *Kramer versus Kramer* syndrome will continue to be more than just movie fiction. In the lives of many husbands and wives, and in the lives of their children, it will be a reality!

CHAPTER FIVE:
THE PARALLELS IMPLIED

"Few doubt the bravery and military skill of General Robert E. Lee. As commander of the Army of Northern Virginia, he was known for shrewdness, fast thinking, an instinct for the counterpunch . . . What many don't know, however, is that Lee had no real taste for war. He much preferred to be at home, romping, playing, and joking with his children, all of whom adored him. The greatest pressure he faced in life was not leading troops, but being away from his family."[1]

"God put our bodies together in such a way that even the parts that seem the least important are valuable. He did this to make all parts of the body work together smoothly, with each part caring about the others. If one part of our body hurts, we hurt all over. If one part of our body is honored, the rest of the body will be honored too."[2]

"MISERY LOVES COMPANY"

We had just returned from a seven-month deployment. In many respects it had been a long and arduous time away from home and loved ones. During the final month of the deployment our ship received a new commanding officer. As our new skipper, he came across as a vibrant, enthusiastic leader who showed genuine concern and regard for the ship's officers and crew. For many of us, this new "C.O." was a refreshing change from the rather dull and dour captain we had previously.

A week after our ship had returned to its home port, the new skipper was sitting at a table in the ship's ward room. Gathered around him were the ship's department heads and the executive officer. There was a serious look on the captain's face—a sign to the "old salts" among us that this was not going to be a typical department head meeting. The C.O. called this meeting to inform us that he was moving on board the ship. What was unusually odd about this announcement was our knowing that most senior officers do not live on board the ship they are assigned to when that ship is in port—*and particularly so if they are married officers with families!*

The captain told us his wife and children had recently moved from another area of the country to the city where our ship was home ported. After a few weeks of living here, the captain had made the decision for his family to move back to where they had previously resided. He pointed out that job and school issues were involved. Therefore, for the remaining eighteen months of his tour, he had decided to move on board the ship. He made it clear that this move was immediate (he had already moved his personal gear into the captain's stateroom), and that this move would have little impact upon the daily routine and atmosphere on board our ship.

In reality, the ship's life and morale were up for significant changes. The captain's demeanor had changed. He no longer came across as enthusiastic, vibrant, and caring as he had been previously. Something had happened in his personal life in terms of his marriage and his family. The captain moved on board as an unhappy and miserable man. For the next year and a half, the ship's company was unhappy and miserable as well. The effect on the captain's personal life had a parallel effect on the ship's life. The result was neither positive nor hopeful.

THE PARALLEL FACTOR IN THE HOSEA MODEL

It was not an easy matter for Hosea to actively seek out his wayward wife—particularly when he saw her as the one who was unfaithful, who left him for other lovers. It was not an easy matter for Hosea to pay a specific price to get back a woman who was "his own" wife. It was not an easy matter for Hosea to attempt to redefine the marriage relationship he had with his wife by using different means and measures. This entire experience, and the process Hosea had to go through as a result, were far from easy. Yet it was by the means of this experience and process that Hosea's vision and understanding changed.

Hosea could make a connection between what was happening in his marriage relationship with his wife and his relationship with God. He began to see a parallel—that many conditions in the relationship with his wife paralleled his relationship with God. When Hosea got back his wife, he had kept his commitment to her. He had paid a price for her. And he had established a standard with her. These very intense and deeply personal experiences helped him to better see and better understand what God was going through in His relationship with the people of Israel.

"In just this way . . .," said Hosea. "In just this way, God would do with the people of Israel similar to what I have done to get back my wife." Hosea saw a connection between what had happened in his own marriage relationship and what was taking place between Israel and God.

THE PARALLEL FACTOR TODAY

Is it possible for us to make connections between our personal relationships and the other relationships that exist in our lives? Is there a parallel factor involved in the health and condition of our intimate relationships and in the well-being of other significant relationships in our lives? The movie actor John Travolta is one who openly admits that this is so. Growing up in a close-knit, Irish-Italian family, Travolta was fortunate to have parents who not only loved him but supported him as he actively sought a career in show business. Highly successful on Broadway, Network Television, and on the Big Screen, at age twenty-six, John Travolta was a successful star whose future was filled with promise and great expectations.

But two traumatic events within a two-year span personally hit Travolta in such a way that it took almost a decade for him to recover. The woman Travolta had passionately fallen in love with, and was the first intense romantic attachment in his life, died from cancer in 1977. Less than two years later, Travolta's mother, his main mentor and advocate, died. During the following decade, John Travolta led a life hidden from the public eye. He faced depression, suffering, and personal grief.

Today, John Travolta is again at the top of his profession. His recent roles in *Pulp Fiction* and in *Get Shorty* have served to revive his career. He is happily married and has a three-year-old son. In a recent interview with *Parade* magazine reporter Dotson Rader, he shares what years of struggle and personal loss have taught him: "I've lost lots of people that I love. But I guess that I have finally learned that when it comes to loving people, you don't have a choice. If you want to feel alive and experience something wonderful, you have to risk great loss. Relationships mean too much to me now to ever walk away."[3]

Personal relationships *do* affect all other relationships in life! The state of health and the condition of our personal relationships affects not only our personal life but also our work life, our public life, and our very outlook on life. When we choose to have meaningful relationships, we choose to take risks—particularly the risks of rejection or loss. However, the joys far outweigh the pains. Relationships force us to get out of our shells and to live not just for ourselves but for others as well. Relationships challenge us to share who we are and what we are with others.

In relationships we get involved with another life besides our own. We share another's sorrows and joys. We celebrate another's strengths. We accept their weaknesses. We learn to express appreciation for what other persons do and to be forgiving for what they fail to do. By being in relationships we learn to accept other persons as they are. We allow them to share with us their intentions, actions, and motives as they define them. This requires us to listen and to be attentive to what others have to say.

Communication becomes not just a forum for telling but also an atmosphere for listening, sharing, learning, and caring.

THE COMMUNICATION BREAKDOWN

In twenty-eight years (eight years in the parish and almost twenty years in the navy) of counseling persons planning to marry, the newly married, and those who have been married for a while, I've noticed a curious phenomenon at work. The longer men and women are in a relationship, the greater the possibility of a communication breakdown. I have never had a couple who were making plans to marry tell me they could not communicate. (In reality, many have said their openness in talking about anything and everything was a major factor in their decision to marry!) Yet I have counseled far too many married couples who have told me that they no longer can communicate.

If personal relationships have such an important part to play in terms of how we view life, and if good communication is vital in keeping such relationships vibrant and constructive, then why the breakdown? If two people initiate a personal relationship with the strong desire and intense willingness to keep their lines of communication open and free flowing, then why, after a few months or a few years of marriage, is it possible for their communication lines to shrivel, shrink, and sag?

The answer lies not so much in the communication itself as it does in the conditions that affect the communication process. It is these conditions that couples need to look at and analyze if they sincerely seek to upgrade their communication skills. In one homework assignment I give to couples, I have them focus their attention on five conditions that affect marital communication. These conditions are expressed in the following five questions:

1. How have I changed?
2. How has the shape of my love changed?
3. How has the level of my respect changed?
4. Where is my level of affection?
5. How do I handle anger and criticism?

How Have I Changed?

People change. They are not the same in the fifth year of a marriage relationship as they were in the beginning of that marriage relationship. They are not the same today as they were six years, six months, or six weeks ago. Their behavior has changed; so have their feelings and ideas. If one wonders why the communication process is different now from what it was, one needs not only to ask, "What has changed?", but specifically, "How have *I* changed?"

How Has the Shape of My Love Changed?

When Ruth first fell in love with Fred, he was her knight in shining armor. He spoke of ideals, hopes, and exciting possibilities. She was thrilled and charmed not only by what he said but how he said it. His abilities and willingness to articulate his thoughts were so clear, concise, and convincing. After five years of marriage, Ruth's knight may not be totally dull, but there are more than a few dents in his armor. Ruth has seen the times when Fred's vision was blurred and impeded, when his moods have kept his thoughts within, and when some of his assets have turned into liabilities. Ruth still loves Fred. However, her familiarity with him has long overtaken what had been the romantic ideal.

How Has the Level of My Respect Changed?

Over the years Ruth has become quite familiar with Fred's various feats and foibles. She is also aware of the qualities and features of Fred's personality that she particularly admires and respects and of those she does not. The level of respect one partner has of the other is a very important condition affecting marital communication. In terms of communication in a relationship, one's level of respect of the other is connected with one's willingness to consider one's partner's point of view.

Where Is My Level of Affection?

The Neil Diamond/Barbra Streisand ballad,"You Don't Bring Me Flowers," speaks volumes concerning this aspect affecting marital communication. If a box of candy or a bouquet of flowers is conducive in helping to end an argument, imagine the effect such presents can have before an argument even begins! Kind acts, words of appreciation, thoughtful gestures, compliments, and little deeds of love can do wonders for the communication process. Harsh remarks, unkind gestures, and neglectful actions can and will do just the opposite. They will serve to build walls and barriers of hurt and resentment that will block, curtail, or severely minimize any real and significant communication between two persons in a relationship.

How Do I Handle Anger and Criticism?

I once worked with a colleague who frequently asked for feedback and assessments on how well he was doing in his work and various responsibilities. After a while, I, along with others who knew him and worked with him, provided less and less feedback instead of more. From our perspective, there were good reasons why this was so. Our colleague viewed any assessments, comments, and responses of his work as criticisms— *negative criticisms.* He wouldn't get angry or outwardly upset. But one could easily tell that he was perturbed. The look on his face alone said a great deal. He would roll his eyes, move his head, lift his voice, and say something like, "Oh, really! Is that right?" Then he would walk away. His voice, his countenance, and his demeanor all gave signs of personal hurt and oversensitivity. His defensiveness and thin-skinned attitude helped to make many of his coworkers feel uncomfortable to be around him. Rather than provide the feedback he said he wanted, they chose to say little or nothing at all. They believed (with just cause from my point of view) that any feedback they would offer would be wrong or be viewed as a personal attack.

Sometimes people find themselves walking on egg shells in terms of their marriage relationships. They are extremely careful in what they say and in what they do for fear that such words and actions will be misunderstood or taken wrong by their partners. Conflict management and conflict resolution become difficult if not impossible processes in marriages where people are extremely sensitive and defensive and are not open to responses and remarks that they do not want to hear. Being thin-skinned is not a desirable trait to have if one desires honest and open communication to take place within a marriage.

CONNECTIONS THAT COUNT!

Our relationship with the one we love parallels our relationship with God. When Hosea got back his wife—when he committed his love to her—when he paid a price for her—when he established a standard with her—he began to see and to understand what God was going through in his relationship with the people of Israel. With all the social upheaval around him, with all the personal upheaval in his own marriage, Hosea could finally proclaim that his people will once again turn to the Lord their God (Hosea 3:5).

What got Hosea to change his view of a condemned people and a condemning God? How was he able to move from despair to hope? From disgust to trust? From "God will show no mercy," to "God will indeed forgive"? What changed Hosea around from experiencing a God of wrath and vengeance to encountering a God of love and mercy was what had taken place within his very own marriage. If Hosea's love could regain a relationship with an unfaithful wife, then most assuredly God's love could restore a relationship with an entire nation of people!

In the New Testament Scriptures this parallel is expressed in terms of Christ and the Church. This is precisely what Paul tells the Christian community at Ephesis: our personal relationships, and in particular our marriage relationships, parallel our relationship with Christ. The Letter to the Ephesians pictures the church as a new social order of love and unity that transcends all social, racial, and ethnic distinctions between people. God, through Christ, calls upon people to be reconciled to himself and to one another. Ephesians 5:22–33 expresses this miracle of restoration and reconciliation through the metaphor of marriage and the relationship that should exist between husbands and wives.

From the Christian perspective, nothing is ever hopeless. People may give up on God, but God never gives up on us. So often in our relationships we want to give up. The tendency is for us to say to ourselves, "Why work on it? It won't do any good. Nothing will change." But how do you know? How do you know, unless you have really tried?

Repeatedly, the Bible shows us in very intimate and personal ways the connections that exist between our relationships with other persons and our relationship with God. All our relationships, particularly our marriage relationships, should never be taken lightly. Relationships have more significance and display more truth than we think they do. This is what Hosea came to realize. This is what Christ revealed. And this is indeed what the community of faith must continue to teach and preach.

CHAPTER SIX:
FINDING RELATIONSHIP MODELS THAT WORK

"The ideas I stand for are not mine. I borrowed them from Socrates. I swiped them from Chesterfield. I stole them from Jesus. And I put them in a book. If you don't like their rules, whose would you use?"[1]

"I solemnly promise and declare that every customer that comes within ten feet of me, I will smile, look them in the eye, and greet them, so help me Sam."[2]

ONE PERSONAL TESTIMONY

The keynote speaker at the National Naval Medical Center's 1996 National Prayer Breakfast was VADM Francis R. Donovan, USN (Ret). As an attendee at that breakfast, I was impressed with two aspects contained in his keynote address. One aspect had to do with Donovan's joining the U.S. Navy at the age of seventeen. Here was an individual who successfully moved up the ranks, from seaman recruit to vice admiral. Yet he never forgot his beginnings in the navy. The second aspect had to do with Donovan's faith in God. He made it quite clear that it was his personal relationship with God that helped him come through the many victories and hardships he encountered throughout his career.

Vice Admiral Donovan pointed out that his desire to be a person of integrity, to seek to treat others with dignity and respect, and to place his life in the hands of God, came from one who had become a significant example in his life—his grandfather. Donovan's grandfather had come from Ireland and as a farmer had toiled daily by cutting hay. He was a big, burley man— a man of prayer. It was this Irish farmer who had become the significant model and inspiration for Vice Admiral Donovan!

WHY MODELS ARE NEEDED

In the biblical book, Ecclesiastes, the author, known as "the Teacher," makes the following observation: "What has been will be again; what has been done will be done again; there is nothing new under the sun. Is there anything of which one can say, 'Look! This is something new. It was here already, long ago; it was here before our time'" (1:9–10) NIV. In his "tell it like it is" forthrightness, the writer of Ecclesiastes makes the case for placing ideas, concepts, and plans in the proper context—which is to not make more of them than what they are. No one idea, concept, or plan is totally new and original. Each one stems from previous ideas, concepts, and plans. Those who would overestimate or overinflate an idea's uniqueness and originality are denying the impact and influence other thoughts and beliefs have played in its formation.

Dale Carnegie knew this to be the case, thus his candid admission declaring his ideas were not original but offshoots from the thinking of others. Sam Walton's approach on how to treat customers was not new by any means. Part of Wal-Mart's success lies in the fact that it was the first large-scale discount store to aggressively treat customers as persons of worth, dignity, and value. Wal-Mart had taken Mom and Pop Shop courtesy and friendliness and effectively put them into super store packaging.

Webster's New World Dictionary (Third College Edition) states that a "model refers to a representation made to be copied or, more general, any person or thing to be followed or imitated because of excellence, worth, etc." If good ideas are copies of other good ideas, then models are representations of persons and things worthy of replication. The account of Hosea's relationship with Gomer and its relevancy to God's relationship with his people is one example of this. It provides a model for relationship formation that is worthy of study, application, and imitation. In a society where there seem to be so very few models of marriage to admire and to imitate in a positive way, the Hosea Model offers us a God-filled and change-inspired choice. The insights one can glean from Hosea's experience may not be earth-shattering or totally new, but when applied to our own relationships they offer insights and truths worthy of emulation.

One does not have to be a marriage counselor to realize that one is living in a land of broken relationships and fractured lives. Nowhere does this phenomenon seem more evident and pronounced than in the area of marriage. In a publication entitled *Marriage In America, a Report to the Nation,* put out by the Council on Families in America in March 1995, it is reported that marriage is an institution in decay: "More people are postponing marriage to older ages, and more people are foregoing marriage altogether . . . While the marriage rate has declined, the divorce rate has climbed to a historically high level—and stayed there. In raw terms, the divorce rate has merely doubled over the past three decades. Yet the probabilities that a marriage will end in divorce have skyrocketed."[3]

What has happened to the state of marriage in the civilian world has had a similar impact within the military community. In 1993, the deputy chaplain of the U.S. Marine Corps made the following startling report: "Although civilian divorce rates have increased slightly since 1980, divorces among Marines over the past twelve years have increased by 76.8% . . . Since a number of remarriages occur when both partners are 'on the rebound' it is not surprising to learn that 40% of military second marriages end in divorce within the first five years of marriage."[4]

At a social function my wife and I attended, we met a woman who was telling us about her twenty-fifth wedding anniversary. As a gift, her husband had given her a necklace and pendent. She went on to share the following account: "Soon after receiving the necklace and pendent, my husband and I attended a party. One lady complimented me on my pendent. When I told her that it was my twenty-fifth wedding anniversary gift, she exclaimed, 'Twenty-five years with the same man? My second marriage didn't even last seven!'"

In the society in which we live, persons married twenty-five years or more are increasingly being looked upon as unusual or even strange. Young people are asking themselves, "Why get into a commitment that will hurt me or cause me difficulty? Perhaps it's best to make no commitments at all!" If we are honest about the current instability of marriages today, perhaps we should rewrite the marriage vows from "to honor and cherish till death do us part" to "I will honor and cherish until my lifestyle is limited— until my partner no longer meets my expectations—until my spouse says or does something I don't like."

What if God's relationship with us hung on many of the same contingencies? If so, you and I would be in dire straits. If so, you and I would be lost causes. Praise the Lord, God *is* God and not like us! God's love for us and God's desire to have a relationship with us are unconditional. This was the message God was communicating to Hosea. It is the same message that needs to be communicated to us today! If it is God's desire and intent that healthy and productive relationships serve as a sign of Divine grace, then what constructive things can persons do within their own relationships to make this so? If health and vitality in a marriage relationship rests on saying and doing the right things and avoiding the saying and doing of wrong things, then the following helpful suggestions come into play.

CREATING THE RIGHT ATMOSPHERE

A certain atmosphere and environment is needed for constructive marital communication and must be in place even before problems, issues, and concerns arise. Three essential "senses" help provide for this. These essential senses are the following:

1. Sense of humor
2. Sense of belonging
3. Sense of little things

Sense of Humor

Charles S. Lauer, the publisher of *Modern Healthcare*, became impressed with how the hiring practices of one of the most successful airlines in the country were connected with the job satisfaction of its employees. Applicants with a sense of humor became prime candidates for employment because they also exhibited positive attitudes. Reflecting on the phenomenon, Lauer states: "You've heard me say it before and I'll say it again: Attitude is everything. I don't care how much education or experience you have, if you don't have a good attitude about yourself and your company you're in trouble. And humor is important in any work environment. It all adds up to healthy morale."[5]

Lauer's comments are as applicable to a relationship between a husband and a wife as they are to a relationship between an employer and an employee. A sense of humor is an essential ingredient in maintaining a healthy, constructive marriage. Being willing and able to laugh at oneself, to see oneself as human and less than perfect, to not be so serious about little things—all serve to make a marriage relationship open, fresh, and vibrantly alive.

The positive power of humor is illustrated in a wonderful and very meaningful devotional that my daughter gave me for Father's Day.

One day Dr. Bernie S. Siegel, author of *Peace, Love and Healing*, got a call from a policeman friend who began talking about all the horrors in the world and about the despair of his own life. He finally said morbidly, "I have nothing to live for. I just called to say good-bye," "Good-bye?" asked Siegel. "What do you mean? The friend said in a monotone voice, "I'm going to commit suicide. I just called to say good-bye." Without a pause, Siegel quipped, "Well, if you do, I'll never speak to you again."

Astounded—and jolted from his deep malaise —the policeman started to chuckle. Instead of shooting himself as he had planned, he decided to go see his friend Bernie for a heart-to-heartefwr chat.

It's very difficult to remain angry at someone who makes you laugh. It's hard to remain sad around a person who makes you giggle. It's extremely difficult to hold a grudge against a person who brings a smile to your face. It's almost impossible to stay frightened if you're with a person who causes you to chuckle. Laughter is a tie that binds hearts together.[6]

Sense of Belonging

I still remember the day I became a boy scout. My mother took me to a neighborhood clothing store to buy me a brand new scout uniform. I even remember my scout neckerchief. It was a drab, brownish, maroon color—not very colorful looking. But it was the neckerchief of *my* troop—Troop 109, Valley Stream, New York! I was given a tenderfoot badge for my mother to sew on the pocket of my new uniform. That night, when I attended the troop meeting, I was directed to a patrol of other scouts—the Moose Patrol (our Moose call was something else!). I was proud. I felt accepted. I was part of a group. I knew I belonged.

A definite strength in my own marriage is the wonderful sense of belonging that my wife and I have in our marriage relationship. We experience a strong connection emotionally, physically, and spiritually. This "togetherness" is not an automatic! The strong sense of belonging we experience in our marriage took years to grow, mature, and develop. My wife, Betty, and I made a conscious and concerted effort to share as much as possible in our work, our play, and in our love. We have always made doing little things together (such as daily walks, talks, small chores, etc.) an important part of our relationship. For we have discovered that its these little things which help keep a marriage dynamic and alive.

Sense of Little Things

A number of years ago, while serving in a pastorate in Connecticut, I signed up for a pastoral counseling program in New York City. It was a program tailored for those working in full time church positions. To participate in the program meant that I had to go into the city for a full day of classes and seminars, once a week, for a two-year period. The church where I served as pastor graciously gave me the time away required to participate in this counseling program. So every Wednesday, I would get up at the crack of dawn, take the commuter train into the city, and be sitting in my first class of the day by 8 AM. Classes would continue until 4 PM. Then I would depart the mental health facility, rapidly walk six blocks to the seminary, where I would take a theologically related course for another two and a half hours. Each Wednesday evening I would arrive home sometime after 9 PM.

Each Wednesday, for two years, while I was away in the city doing my own thing, my wife had numerous responsibilities of her own to take care of— including a couple of small children to look after and care for. For both my wife and me, those two years were difficult and stressful ones. In spite of the difficulties of that time, I remember one particular little thing that helped us cope. Each Wednesday evening, when I finally got home, the children were already in bed. My wife and I would sit down to a 10 PM candlelight meal. It was our special time together to eat a meal and share our day. Today, I may have trouble remembering the courses I took during that intensive two-year counseling program. But I have never forgotten those wonderful candlelight dinners!

I share this experience to point out how important little things can be in a marriage relationship. Wednesday night candlelight dinners were not only a wonderful way for my wife and me to relax and unwind after a stress-filled day; they also provided a time of tranquility and intimacy that we both needed. Ten o'clock became a time not only to quietly end a hectic Wednesday, it also became a time to quietly put away an entire week of busyness, frustrations, and interruptions.

Marriages need such times to serve to unwind frustrations, unload stress, and relieve pressures. Husbands and wives need words of encouragement, words of appreciation, affectionate greetings, family celebrations, and small and unexpected acts of kindness and consideration. A sense of little things helps to undergird and uplift a marriage and keep the relationship responsible and responsive.

KEEPING THE MARRIAGE ALIVE

In order for marriages to grow stronger and better, more is needed in addition to the right atmosphere and environment. Certain habits and priorities also need to be established and faithfully practiced. What are these habits and priorities? Four items in particular are worthy of consideration.

Spend time together, alone! I recently counseled a senior officer who was anxiously facing impending retirement from the military. From his point of view, the future looked dim and bleak rather than bright and beautiful. He had not made any plans for the transition from military to civilian life. In addition to career change, he also was facing family change. His children had recently finished schooling and had left the family nest. Now it was just he and his wife who were facing a new life together. When I asked him when was the last time he and his wife had gone on a vacation, he responded that it was almost four years ago, and at that time it was a trip to visit relatives. I then asked him when was the last time he and his wife had gotten away together for a weekend. He couldn't remember when that last time was.

Dates do not end with marriage! Couples need time to unwind, recreate, play, rest and relax together. If couples do not consciously and conscientiously make the time necessary to be together socially, recreationally, and intimately, they are more likely to face the reality of a deadened and perhaps even dead end marriage.

Rearrange family schedules! The "Father Knows Best" and the "Leave It To Beaver" images of one spouse working, the other spouse staying at home, and the entire household regularly gathered together for evening meals, are far more fantasy than reality today. Husbands and wives face conflicting work schedules, time schedules, and numerous other obstacles that play havoc with their desire to have meaningful relationships.

Who has the con (control) on family time, you or the schedule? In a recent TV show a man tells his estranged wife that he can't take their son camping on the weekend as he had promised due to a change in business plans. "Tell him it's business," he pleads to his ex-wife, as he heads out the door. "He'll understand." "That's what's wrong," replies the estranged wife.

"You've always made the decision to place business over time with your son!"

Conflicts and conflicting priorities are always going to play havoc with our family schedules. But sensitivity to the needs of those we love, and creativity in arranging important times to be with the ones we love, are crucial to the well-being of such relationships if they are to thrive as well as survive.

Put your marriage first! Genesis 2:23–24 NIV states the following: "The man said, 'This is now bone of my bone and flesh of my flesh; she shall be called [woman], for she was taken out of man.' For this reason a man will leave his father and mother and be united to his wife, and they will become one flesh." This is the biblical way of saying that a man is to hold on to his wife and not on to his parents or his children.

A marriage involves a union, a bonding, and a joining of two people. In a marriage relationship, two persons "become one flesh." Such a relationship requires and necessitates a priority and an importance not found in other human relationships. Children are important. But as they grow and mature, they have their own lives to lead and their own relationships to form. We are not married to our children. The lifelong commitment required in a marriage between a man and a woman involves a priority not found anywhere else (with the exception of one's relationship to God). Neither are we married to our parents. The person who puts his or her parents before his or her spouse has sown the seeds of marital dischord and disharmony.

Check what is at the center of your marriage! A Hasidic story tells of a small boy playing hide-and-seek with his friends. For some unknown reason, the other children stopped playing and left while the boy was still hiding. At not being found, the child began to cry. His grandfather came out of the house to see what had happened. After learning the child's predicament, the grandfather said, "Don't weep, my child, because the boys did not come to find you. Perhaps you can learn a lesson from this disappointment. All of life is like a game between God and us. Only it is God who is weeping, for we are not playing the game fairly. God is waiting to be found, but many have gone in search of other things."[7]

Where is God in your marriage? Is God at the center and very core of the relationship you have with your spouse? Or is God at the periphery? Can God even be found in your marriage? Is the spiritual dimension of your marriage like a game—a game of hide-and-seek where God has yet to be found? The significance and impact the Hosea Model can have in marriage rests upon a very important truth: God was at the very center of Hosea's marriage. The insights and truths that Hosea received regarding commitment, cost, standard, and parallel relationships were due to the fact that Hosea kept God at the center of his marriage.

THE MODEL OF HOSEA REVISITED

As a man, Hosea spoke through his own human experience. As God's prophet, Hosea also spoke through Divine experience. Like the communication of other biblical prophets, Hosea's message stressed the futility of pursuing idols and on depending upon the support and goodwill of foreign powers instead of depending upon God. But because his own marriage was at stake, the words of Hosea convey particular heartfeltness and personal struggle. While it is certainly the case that other prophets resorted to numerous methods in their struggle to help restore God's people to their true faith, the communication of Hosea was unique. He alone conveyed how the personal relationship of his marriage related to God's relationship with God's people. This is why many rabbinic scholars view Hosea as a new type of prophet—one who spoke in conventional relationship terms to the individual as well as to the community.[8]

The story of Hosea's marriage offers those of us who sincerely desire to strenghten and make better our own marriage relationships more than just a model to use. Hosea's story also provides a personal message of love, hope, and relationship redemption. Hosea presents a God who conveys "the strong love of a Father, the tender love of a mother, and the true love of a husband."[9] Hosea presents a God who is real in the sense that this God even cares about our most personal and intimate relationships. It is this very same God who wants to enter our lives and relationships to provide blessings and benefits that we can never find on our own. It is when we allow this God to enter into our marriage and all other aspects of our lives that we become different people—people who experience a difference that makes all the difference in the world!

APPENDIX:

FOUR HOMEWORK ASSIGNMENTS THAT HELP COUPLES FOCUS, COMMUNICATE, AND GROW IN THEIR RELATIONSHIPS

Over the years, as I've worked with couples planning to marry or already married, I have developed specific homework assignments for them to take home and work on individually and then share together as a couple. As a chaplain and as a counselor I have found these homework assignments to be helpful in a number of ways. First, since it is a practice of mine in both premarital and marital counseling to see a couple four to five times over a series of weeks, homework assignments provide couples with a constructive tool to use between counseling sessions. Second, homework assignments help place the emphasis and the work on the couples themselves rather than on me as the counselor "guru" or the "answer man." Third, these assignments provide couples with focused communication tools—communication tools that focus on their relationships. These tools help couples see where their relationship problems and issues really are and challenge them to discuss (and hopefully make) the changes needed to make their relationships better, stronger, and more honest.

The first three homework assignments follow the same format and procedure. Toward the end of my counseling session with a couple, I hand each a copy of homework assignment #1, #2, or #3, depending on the area of concern in the relationship to be covered during the next session with the couple. They are instructed to take the homework assignment home, carefully read it, and answer the questions raised by writing their responses down in a notebook or a piece of paper. In answering each question they are to be as honest and as candid as possible. In responding to each question they are to answer in terms of themselves and where they are in their relationship. They are not to answer for their partner or where they think their partner is in terms of the question or the relationship. In other words, they are the "expert" on their own selves in terms of their own personal feelings and thoughts as it relates to each question raised within the assignment. They are instructed to spend at least forty-five minutes to an hour on each homework assignment. They are to answer the questions alone, by themselves, and without discussion or help from their partner. When a couple have both completed the assignment, they are to pick a specific and special time for discussion and feedback. The time picked must be a "neutral time"—that is, a time not caught up in the hustle and bustle of other things and other priorities. It is a time mutually agreed upon by the couple in which they can and will focus all their attention on the discussion of the assignment at hand. They are not tired, emotionally drained, argumentative, upset, bothered by interruptions from children, family, friends, or called away by the telephone or by other concerns. This neutral time should last at least for one hour, if not longer. The couple is to take turns reading or sharing their response to each question with their partner. After a particular question has been answered by both persons then they are to discuss their answers and their reactions to the other's answers with each other. When they feel the topic at hand as been adequately discussed they then move on to the next question and repeat the process all over again.

Homework assignment #4 challenges a couple to look at a lifestyle, to develop habits, and build a foundation that will enable them to deal with conflicts in their relationship in constructive rather than destructive ways. It is an assignment to provoke and stimulate serious thought and consideration by the couple in terms of where they presently are and where they may desire to be regarding the health, well-being, and maturity of their marriage relationship.

HOMEWORK ASSIGNMENT #1

The following six questions deal with key issues concerning the relationship of marriage. These are not the usual questions that couples focus attention on when preparing themselves for marriage. However, once married, couples discover these questions have great relevance because the issues they address are very important and very real!

Take your time in answering each question (forty-five minutes is not too long!). Be honest and truthful in your response. Write your answer down so you will remember it and be able to read it and share it with your partner. Answer each question from the perspective of yourself in terms of this relationship. Remember you are the expert on you.

Once you have answered all six questions, and your partner has done the same, determine a time, place, and environment suitable for sharing responses. The minimum time to do this is one hour. The place to do this is mutually determined by both of you. It should be a place where you will not be interrupted by outside factors such as television, telephone, messages, or other people. The environment should be devoid of anything that would cause hassle, stress, or tension.

Take turns answering each question. When both of you have answered a question, spend some time discussing your responses. When you both feel this has been done then move on to the next question. Remember that both of you should respond to the same question before taking the time to discuss your individual responses.

Six Important Questions to Ask Within the Context of a Marriage Relationship

1. What degree of freedom should you have within your relationship? And how do you define that freedom?

2. How do you see yourself, in terms of who you are as a person, within this relationship?

3. How much do you understand the feelings and priorities of the other person in this relationship?

4. How flexible are you within your relationship in terms of crises, past mistakes and hurts?

5. How creative are you within this relationship? To what extent do you try new ways or go in new directions?

6. What degree of trust exists within this relationship? How much do you trust yourself? To what extent do you trust your partner?

HOMEWORK ASSIGNMENT #2

The relationship of marriage takes work—constant work! Unlike the wedding that precedes it, it is never a done deal. Taking such into account, the *vital* question to ask is this: *Do you want to make your marriage grow?* Marriages grow when five important steps take place:

1. Two people develop a sense of concern for each other. They *actually* and *actively* care about one another.
2. Two people learn to listen to each other. They really share their feelings.
3. Two people begin to speak straight. They are honest and truthful with each other.
4. Two people make a contract with each other. They are committed to work on this relationship.
5. Two people agree to work on the dimensions of marriage. (The homework assignment is based on this fifth step.)

The Eight Dimensions of a Healthy Marriage

A healthy marriage is multi-dimensional. If you were to score yourself in each of the following eight dimensions concerning the relationship of marriage, what would your score be? Analyze and evaluate yourself in terms of the relationship you have with your partner in the following eight dimensions. On each dimension give yourself a score from 1 to 10; 1 being the lowest and 10 being the highest. The more truthful and honest you are the more you will get out of this assignment. Remember you are scoring yourself and not your partner. After you have written down your responses find a suitable time to share your answers with your partner.

1. *The Emotional Dimension:* How aware are you of the other's feelings and being able to tune in to where they are coming from? What score would you give yourself and why?
2. *The Creative Dimension:* How good are you at sharing and working as a team with your partner in a variety of areas? What would your score be and why?
3. *The Social Dimension:* How well do you share with your partner in recreation and play? Your score and why?
4. *The Intellectual Dimension:* How well do you share in the world of ideas with your partner? Your score and why?
5. *The Sexual Dimension:* How well do you share in sexual satisfaction and emotional fulfillment with your partner? Your score and why?

6. *The Religious Dimension:* How well do you share the meaning of life with your partner? Your score and why?

7. *The Covenantal Dimension:* How well do you stand through crises and conflict with your partner? Your score and why?

8. *The Legal Dimension:* How well do you share the written contract of responsibility with your partner? Your score and why?

HOMEWORK ASSIGNMENT #3

In marriage, couples usually point to communication as one of the key problems within their relationship. Why is this so? Communication is far more than talking. It actually covers all aspects of a marriage relationship: family, finances, friends, sex, job, etc. Why is it that prior to marriage couples don't appear to have problems communicating but after marriage (years, months, weeks, and even days into it) they do?

Over time in a personal relationship such as marriage things change and so do people. You are not the same person you were when you began your relationship with your partner as you are now. There are certain key factors that affect marital communication. Five of these factors are listed below. Your assignment is to individualize these factors by asking yourself five questions. The more candid and frank your assessment of yourself in terms of each of these factors, the more you can learn about the art and complexity of marital communication. Again, after completing this assignment find a suitable time to share your responses with your partner.

Factors Affecting Marital Communication

1. Change and growth of a person in terms of feelings, behavior, and ideas affects communication. The question to ask yourself: How have I changed?
2. Change in the shape of love as one moves from romance to familiarity affects communication. The question to ask: How has my love changed during this relationship?
3. Change in the level of respect—specifically one's willingness to consider the other's point of view, affects communication. The question to ask: How has my level of respect changed?
4. The level of affection (is it up or down?). The question to ask: Where is my level of affection?
5. Handling anger and criticism (how sensitive or defensive am I?). The question to ask: How well do I handle anger and criticism?

Testing Your Communication

If the following comments were made to you, how would you feel?

"I know what you think!"

"You always do what you want!"

"If you cared about me you wouldn't do this!"

"You're selfish!"

The above are examples of overgeneralization or moving from communication to total war. Assumption is the rule. There is another way. It involves checking out meaning. Whenever communication becomes blurred, confused, or heated, something is mixed up in the process. It is your responsibility to help clear confused communication. This is done by stating what you think and feel (Use "I" statements and avoid "you" statements). Be clear. Ask, "What do you mean?" And ask for feedback. Ask, "What did you hear me say?" Or "What did you think I'm saying?"

HOMEWORK ASSIGNMENT #4

Conflict is an inevitable fact within the dynamics of any marriage relationship. The clashing of ideas, wills, and points of view, disagreements in terms of personal interests and ideas, and emotional disturbances resulting from opposing impulses are part and parcel of what can and does take place within interpersonal relationships. It is part of the turf that goes with any marriage. This homework assignment does not challenge the reality or the validity of conflict within marriage. But it does raise the question as to whether one chooses to make much of the conflict within one's marriage *constructive* or *destructive*.

Destructive Conflict

Destructive conflict can destroy persons as well as marriages! Many times destructive conflict in a marriage is the result of false assumptions. Two ways false assumptions are made are through *skin-jumping* and *mind-reading*.

Skin-jumping: Occurs when one person assumes they know what the other person is thinking.

"I *know* what's really going through your mind!"

"I *know* what you really mean behind those words!"

Mind-reading: Occurs when one assumes the other knows or should know what one is thinking.

"You *know what I* go through!"

"You *know what I* mean!"

"You *know how I* feel!"

We *cannot* mind-read or skin-jump. We do not know what another person is thinking and feeling. We cannot tell another person what he or she should think or feel. We can only ask someone what he is thinking or feeling. We only know what they choose to tell us. Each person is the best authority on himself or herself in terms of their feelings and thoughts.

Whenever conflict in marriage is viewed only as negative and destructive, it is usually dealt with in one of three ways:

1. *The Murder Approach*: We are going to have an argument. It's imperative that I win and you lose. So I take out my imaginary shotgun and blow you away. End of argument and end of conflict.

2. *The Suicide Approach*: We are going to have an argument. It seems like you always win and I always lose. I don't want to give you the satisfaction of blowing me away so I will get out my symbolic sword and commit ritual suicide. End of argument and end of conflict.

3. *The Avoid The Whole Issue Approach*: We are going to have an argument. I hate arguments, disputes, and conflicts of any kind and so do you. Let's both ignore the problem and maybe it will go away.

Constructive Conflict

Conflict in marriage can be constructive. One can grow, learn, and improve as a result of conflict, and so can a marriage relationship. But this involves a mind set, a view of life, and a way of living that helps see life, people, and events in positive and creative ways. How is this done? There are three essential "senses" that if put into practice can help this come about.

1. *Having a Sense of Humor*: Are you willing and able to laugh at yourself? How willingly? How frequently? Are you able to keep little things little, or are they blown out of proportion? Can you accept the humanity of others as well as of yourself? The regular practice of a sense of humor helps make a marriage fresh and open.

2. *Having a Sense of Belonging*: To what extent in your marriage do you share in work, play, and love? How frequently and in what ways do you do little things together? A strong sense of belonging is what helps keep a marriage vibrant and alive.

3. *Having a Sense of Little Things*: Little things *do* mean a lot! How often and in what ways are words of appreciation, affectionate greetings, and family celebrations given in your marriage? Having a real sense of little things undergirds a marriage and keeps it flexible.

Keeping the Marriage Alive

There are also key habits one can build and develop within marriage that create and promote vitality and aliveness for the relationship. Four important ones are the following:

1. *Spend Time Together, Alone!*: Are there regular and specific times reserved for you and your spouse? How often do you take walks together, go to the movies together, spend special time together? Dates don't end with marriage!

2. *Rearrange Family Schedules!*: A birthday, an anniversary, or a special event does not always have to be missed. It can be scheduled around, and, if not, it can be rearranged. Do you practice creativity and flexibility in your marriage relationship? Remember it is you who can get into ruts. Ruts do not get into you!

3. *Put Your Marriage First!*: "A man leaves his father and mother and cleaves to his wife" (Genesis 2:24). This is the biblical way of saying that a man is to hold onto his wife, not his parents or his children. What and who are the real priorities in your life? Are your marriage and your spouse anywhere on the top of your list?

4. *Check What Is at the Center of Your Marriage!*: Is God there? And if not, why not? Where *is* God in your marriage? Is your marriage foundation built on "solid rock" or is it more like "sinking sand"?

In the movie *The Preacher's Wife*, the angel asks the preacher's wife the following question: "What do you do when the flame goes out of your marriage?" As she takes a moment to seriously wrestle with the question, the angel replies, "The right answer is: Don't let it!" BE A KEEPER OF THE FLAME!

NOTES

INTRODUCTION

1. The Order for the Service of Marriage, 1965, *The Methodist Publishing House,* Nashville, Tenn., p. 28

CHAPTER TWO

1. Bernard Meltzer, *Bernard Meltzer's Guidance For Living* (New York: Signet Books, 1982), p. 112.
2. The movie was entitled *Leave of Absence,* and starred Brian Dennehy, Blythe Danner, and Jacqueline Bisset. This film, made in 1994, was shown on the NBC Monday Night Movie on July 24, 1995.
3. *Love in Difficult Relationships,* by Gary Rosberg, Ed.D. (The American Association of Christian Counselors Counsel Tapes, 1994).
4. Sidney Harris, *Detroit Free Press* (November 21, 1966).
5. Alan Bullock, *Hitler and Stalin* (Alfred A. Knoph: New York, 1992). This is particularly evident in Chapter Ten, where the personal lives and relationships of Stalin and Hitler are compared. Bullock describes Stalin as a man "who had become walled up in himself, possessed by the role he had assumed, and incapable of responding to human affection" (p. 376). Hitler is described as "an archetypal 'loner,'" and as one who had a "contemptous attitude toward women" (pp. 376–77).
6. M. Scott Peck, *The Road Less Traveled* (Touchstone Books: New York, New York, 1985), p. 92.
7. Soren Kierkegaard. *The Journals of Kierkegaard;* Ed. By Alexander Dru (Harper & Row: New York, 1959), p. 92.
8. Peck, *The Road,* p. 140.
9. Lawrence O. Richards, *Expository Dictionary of Bible Words* (Regency Reference Library: Zondervan Publishing House: Grand Rapids, Michigan, 1985), p.194.
10. Psalm 119 is a biblical hymn to this reality. As the Psalm so eloquently shows, it takes the entire Hebrew alphabet to attempt to describe God's Precepts, Promises, and Laws.

CHAPTER THREE

1. Jo Carr and Imogene Sorely, *Bless This Mess* (Abingdon Press: Nashville, 1984) p. 41.
2. Ephesians 5:21–33 specifically refers to husband and wife relationships. However, the marriage relationship is only one example of the new standards and new relationships expected between those persons who follow Christ.

CHAPTER FOUR

1. Source unknown.
2. A letter to the editor written by Michael Morse in the excerpt from "Letters" section of *The Washington Post Magazine*, August 13, 1995, p. 3.
3. John L. Thomas, S.J., *Beginning Your Marriage*, seventh edition (ACTA Publications: Chicago, Ill., 1987), p. 88. An eighth edition of this book, revised by David M. Thomas, Ph.D, was published in 1994 with expanded sections on interfaith and interethnic marriages.
4. Karen Gould, *Grace Notes*, Nov. 95, p. 6. Published by Grace United Methodist Church, 119 N. Frederick Ave., Gaithersburg, Md.

CHAPTER FIVE

1. *God's Little Devotional Book For Dads* (Honor Books, Inc.: Tulsa, Oklahoma, 1995), p. 111.
2. I Corinthians 12:24b–26 CEV.
3. Dotson Rader, "You Have To Let Your Heart Be Someone Else's Heart," *Parade Magazine*, October 22, 1995, p. 6.

CHAPTER SIX

1. Quote attributed to Dale Carnegie.
2. The employee pledge of Wal-Mart discount stores.
3. This report was sponsored by the Institute for American Values, p. 7.
4. CDR E.T. Gomulka, CHC, USN, "Marriage and Military Life," *MARINES*, September 1993, p. 7.
5. Charles S. Lauer, "Publisher's Letter," *Modern Healthcare*, January 15, 1996.
6. *God's Little Devotional Books for Dads* (Honor Books, Inc.: Tulsa, Oklahoma, 1995) p. 87.
7. Paul Wharton, *Stories and Parables for Preachers and Teachers* (Paulist Press: New York, 1986) p. 12.
8. Dr. Shalom Coleman, *Hosea Concepts in Midrash and Talmud* (Block Publishing: New York, 1960), p. 46.
9. Ibid., p. 46.